When No One Leads the Church

When No One Leads the Church

*Pastoral Leadership and the Formation
of a Healthy Church Culture*

❧

REGINALD W. STEELE

Foreword by Kenneth N. Ngwa

WIPF & STOCK · Eugene, Oregon

WHEN NO ONE LEADS THE CHURCH
Pastoral Leadership and the Formation of a Healthy Church Culture

Copyright © 2025 Reginald W. Steele. All rights reserved. Except for brief quotations in critical publications or reviews, no part of this book may be reproduced in any manner without prior written permission from the publisher. Write: Permissions, Wipf and Stock Publishers, 199 W. 8th Ave., Suite 3, Eugene, OR 97401.

Wipf & Stock
An Imprint of Wipf and Stock Publishers
199 W. 8th Ave., Suite 3
Eugene, OR 97401

www.wipfandstock.com

PAPERBACK ISBN: 979-8-3852-4752-3
HARDCOVER ISBN: 979-8-3852-4753-0
EBOOK ISBN: 979-8-3852-4754-7

All Scriptures unless otherwise noted are from the New Revised Standard Version Bible, copyright © 1989 National Council of the Churches of Christ in the United States of America. Used by permission. All rights reserved worldwide.

Scriptures marked NIV are taken from the New International Version® (NIV®). Copyright © 1973, 1978, 1984, 2011 by Biblica, Inc. Used by permission of Zondervan.

I dedicate this volume to the African American Baptist Church community, of which I am a part. Additionally, I extend this dedication to my family, encouraging colleagues, and friends who have stood by me throughout the creation of this work, as well as to those who have paved the way before me.

Contents

Foreword by Kenneth N. Ngwa ix

Introduction xi

1   The Formation of Survival Modalities 1
2   Social Origins of Family Legacy Group Members 19
3   Teaching as a Tool for Transformation 36
4   Right Beliefs and Behaviors for the Congregation and Her Leader 52
5   Lent and Pilgrimage : Congregational Practices that Lead to Transformation 70
6   Transforming 87
7   Transformation's Impact on Congregational and Social Arenas 104

   Conclusion 121

   Bibliography 131

Foreword

Kenneth N. Ngwa

In *When No One Leads the Church*, Reginald Steele addresses the intersectional social and spiritual work of the practice of leadership in the (Black Baptist) church. Steele's is a voice from inside, calling the church to engage in reflection about such important matters as power and leadership, power struggle in times of transition, and the spiritual and social work necessary to generate an ethic of communal belonging that is both disruptive to ideologies of singular or "exclusive" power structures and identities and generative for unending inclusive visioning of the modes and manners of liberative leadership and communal flourishing. His interest in bridging gaps—between academia and church, between the mind and the heart, between the classroom and the street, between orthodoxy and orthopraxis—has developed out of a desire to be fully authentic in his voice as a Black man, a Christian, and a pastor called to engage and interpret religious texts and traditions of faith in ways that inform, transform, and inspire. The cost of such work, the labor involved, the capacity for internal fraying, and for communal resilience and ultimate flourishing require more than a casual assessment of the strategies of community survival, which can function in oppositional ways to initiatives of change.

Over several years, I have had the delight of talking with Reggie about the levels and layers of mutual transformation that animate the lives of church leaders and members around the shared experience of the church as an institution. History and historiography inform social identity, spiritual commitments, and direction. In that long history and historiography, the church's identity and mission intersect with that of its leader. To belong to a church is not just a matter of spiritual and social practice; it is also a matter of identity and transformational formation, affirmation of self-worth, and a commitment to liberation. To be a leader in a church is, in some ways, also a matter of the same. When transitional moments arrive, tensions may arise. Steele offers a richly nuanced analysis and perspective on such moments; first, by naming the power struggles that often animate those moments and create survival modes of existence, and second, by offering a pedagogical way forward.

What if, instead of being stuck in a perpetual cycle and mode of survival, one commits to a pilgrimage, a pedagogy, a praxis, and a spirituality of transformation in the service of personal, communal, and institutional thriving? This spirituality, which requires self-reflection and dialogue, creates the opportunity to engage—from a position of plenitude rather than deficiency—the social and spiritual traumas that the church seeks to name and overcome. In this journey, Steele makes a daring but deeply spiritual move, stepping outside of the theological and institutional space of the Black church into the world of Islam through the life story of Malcolm X. This is not a voyeuristic journey nor is it casual interreligious analogizing; rather, Steele proposes such a journey as spiritual practice that opens one to curiosity and self-reflection that mitigate against the dangers and risks of entrenched ideologies and practices that cast harmful and deleterious effects on the ministry of the church. A church that does not have or develop the capacity for robust internal self-examination, critical reflection, and partnership-building may very well be on its way toward normalizing unethical or limiting faith—a faith that revolves around survival. What if resurrection is a real alternative, available to both the church and to all who seek to lead it?

Introduction

EXPERIENCE AND ENCOUNTER ARE the crucibles that shape what groups deem particular within a given context. In most cases, the characteristics that define a group are not problematic. Instead, they serve as a proverbial identification card, showing how a specific group sees themselves, e.g., race, class, gender, inclusionary markers, preference, and neighborhood of residence. When a group's character trait is established, the created image becomes a marker by which a group is seen within a given social construct. However, the results of a group's options can sometimes appear opposing when extended beyond a set period. This is why it is crucial, indeed fascinating, to delve into a group's social experiences. Understanding these experiences is not just a scholarly pursuit but a gateway to understanding why they function, exist, believe what they believe, and behave how they behave.

First, consider an urban Black Baptist church as our working example. For the book's sake, we will call it Wayside Baptist Church. Wayside certainly has a history of challenges, and two variables remain central to their experience: transient leadership and congregational conflict. Throughout Wayside's history, leadership disassociations fostered congregational traumas. As a result, members who remained at the church created a congregational culture necessary to sustain the church.

When I speak of a "congregational culture" in the context of the Wayside Baptist Church, I am not merely referring to a set of beliefs. I am alluding to an intricate system of ideas and practices that the church members have meticulously crafted. In this book,

Introduction

I often use the terms "survival modalities" and "survival mode dynamics" as more nuanced substitutes for the term "congregational culture." This fostered culture, often shaped by leaders during times of transition, has not only influenced church members but also intricately woven into the church's social dynamics, even if they don't always align with the church's official rules and regulations.

In this book, I categorize the group responsible for creating this nuanced congregational culture as family legacy group (FLG) members. They are not just a collective group of individuals in the church but a testament to the power of community. Through their shared vision and determination, they seek to sustain control and influence over the doings of the congregation. Their association at the inception of their formation was not based on blood ties. Still, over time, familial bonds and shared experiences have forged a unity and strength that has made them a formidable force in the church. The unwavering unity and stability of the family legacy group within the church vividly demonstrate the power of community, a testament to their commitment and dedication.

With constant periods of congregational conflicts and vacant pulpits, this group developed a set of skills that were used to settle the congregation. While newer members dealt with the perceptions and traumas associated with the changes in the church, FLG members forged an identity of their own. Sandra L. Barnes, in *Black Church Culture and Community Action*, writes, "Cultural theory posits that social groups possess a cultural repertoire or tool kit that reflects beliefs, ritual practices, stories, and symbols that provide meaning and impetus for resource mobilization."[1] For members of the Wayside Baptist Church's family legacy group, their created system exists as their "toolkit," used for fixing what they assessed was broken and dismantling what they did not want built.[2]

Generally, groups within Black Baptist churches that function as FLGs engage in social behaviors seeking to sustain and preserve their way of congregational life. How their beliefs and

---

1. Barnes, "Black Church Culture," 967–94.
2. Barnes, "Black Church Culture," 967–94.

INTRODUCTION

behavior impact those within a given space, whether positive or negative in their expression, is often not considered. While family legacy groups are not exclusive to Black Baptist churches, my framing of congregational challenges is exclusive to my congregational experiences. Sustainability and survival are the motivating factors for this faction within a congregational context. When survival cultural contexts exist beyond a temporal period, they become distorted. The continuation of a distorted ideology often manifests an ethic interpreted as oppositional. For several Black Baptist churches, this medium serves as a congregational epidemic that hinders progression on many levels.

One contrasting perspective to my theory exists: who determines who is right and who is wrong? Most Black Baptist churches have a system of governance and functioning that predates the consistent adoption of the FLG's survival modality. In churches like Wayside, the governing system is perceived as the system of the church because most of the church leaders are either members of the family legacy group or influenced by the family legacy group. Often, the desires for alteration come from new congregational leaders. And, if what they seek to present aligns itself with the status quo, their ideas are embraced. If what they show is antithetical to the created ideology, resistance ensues and steps are taken to encourage congregational disassociation.

How do we distinguish rightness and congregational anarchy in Black Baptist churches? It is easy to suggest that these survival modalities created by the faction are flawed. Consequently, if there is no direct pushback from church members, can this system that functions as the guiding governance of the church be identified as contradictory or even combative to what is understood as an established governance of the church? If so, by what measure is it tested against? If not, how does a church ground itself when alterations to what they believe and how they live out their beliefs change based on influential members of the FLG? How does one determine the correct polity, governance, and practice in this context?

Although this newly created system may not directly align with the established polity and practices of the church, it moves

INTRODUCTION

the church along during transitional periods. In these moments, survival mode dynamics are necessary for congregational sustainability. Conflicts occur in the Black Baptist church when pastoral positions are filled. The tensions associated with ratifying survival modalities often speak more to power and influence over polity and practice, thus causing oppositional behavioral practices geared toward keeping things as they are instead of experiencing restructuring and congregational transformation. For some, the result is congregational anarchy. For others, this moment of transition serves as a potential catalyst for change. This is the essence of the work.

What is the impact on the church when created modalities are no longer needful but now exist as a congregational norm? What happens to a congregation when something that once was necessary now exists as something oppositional? Is a traditional set of rules the benchmark for correctness in congregational/social spaces? Each situation requires individual evaluation based on the context in which the traditional/established ideology functions. For example, on a societal level, white supremacy is the original intent and precise position of the traditional/established ideology framing the US Constitution in America. According to this conventional system, African Americans would be considered the contrary group based on their contradiction of the original intent of the social construct of whiteness by claiming full human dignity and equality as a minority group in America. How do we make proper distinctions? Whose system do we follow?

Suppose the traditional/established rules are the status quo in this example. In that case, everyone who represents "the other" is indirectly encouraged to assess themselves based on the status quo of whiteness, e.g., white particularity claimed as the norm for full humanity (racism), male particularity claimed as the norm for full humanity (androcentrism/sexism), straight/cis particularity claimed as the norm for full humanity (heteronormativity/homophobia), and able-bodied particularity claimed as the norm for full humanity (ableism). Suppose the traditional/established system does not serve the best interest of all. In that case, a new

INTRODUCTION

system is essential to the masses, and the traditional/established system needs altering. However, if reintroducing the established system fosters opportunities for growth, restructuring, and congregational/community expansion, then I assert that the established system be considered and evaluated.

I suggest that any system created that extends itself beyond the parameters of its needfulness is contradictory and out of order. Additionally, those representing themselves as family legacy group members in Black Baptist churches seeking to superimpose their created system should work with the selected leader to improve the church and community. I will reference a specific leadership experience in a particular Black Baptist church as an example of this problem that I believe to be at work in the case of family legacy groups in the Black Baptist church, which I want to address and remedy.

In several Black Baptist churches, sustained systems of power and controlling practices administered by FLGs foster tensions if lived out beyond their needfulness. In referencing a specific congregational context, the right system to follow may be the established/traditional system created and agreed upon by the collective body. For clarification, my assertion of an established system of congregational governing and practice does not seek to embrace or reject a conservative ministry methodology. Whether traditional, moderate, or progressive in its forms, methods of ministry presentation and structures should have a foundation they stand on that best represents the divine mission of Jesus. Related to my congregational experiences, I have watched FLG members live out a system of created ideals antithetical to the established system of rules in the church and align their human behavior in ways that negatively impact a congregation's attempts to develop transformation and communal mutuality.

In assessing what I have described as an issue that negatively impacts the Black Baptist church, I wish to offer an unconventional solution to what some deem as a common problem in the Black Baptist church. With this understanding, I seek to look to the lived experiences and encounters of Malcolm X during the periods of

Introduction

pre-hajj and pilgrimage as an example comparable to the problems in the Black Baptist church, surrounding issues relating to tensions concerning systems of understanding, practice, and social behaviors assessed as oppositional based on a singular group's desire to maintain power and control.

This comparison between Malcolm X's experience and the family legacy group dynamics in the Black Baptist church will traverse itself through seven chapters in the book: the formation of survival modalities, the social origins of family legacy group members, teaching as a tool for transformation, right belief and behavior for the congregation and her leader, lent and pilgrimage as a practice towards transformation, transforming, and transformation's impact on congregational and social arenas.

In chapter 1, I compare Malcolm X, the Nation of Islam, and the FLG in ways that speak to the formation of survival modalities. Using his pre-hajj period will provide an analogy of how, in the Black Baptist congregation, ideologies interpreted as contrasting to an established/traditional interpretation of system structures and practices contribute to behaviors lived out in oppositional ways. While these survival mode dynamics empower the social identity of the family legacy group, they are perceived as antithetical to the established/traditional polity and prevent the congregation from the kind of mutual, participatory, democratic processes and practices created by the larger body.

In chapter 2, I foster awareness of the social origins of family legacy groups. The goal is not to establish a right or wrong analysis but to encourage an understanding of the group's social makeup and congregational experiences that may have pushed them into survival mode. While education is essential throughout, this stage is dedicated to creating a safe space for awareness, comfort, and, eventually, social acceptance. To better comprehend how social conditions impact continued beliefs and behaviors that stray from traditional faith, we will explore the lived experiences and encounters of Malcolm X and the Nation of Islam.

In chapter 3, I delve into the influence of religious teachings and explore how regular participation, education, application, and

Introduction

external support systems beyond the local church can transform individuals within their family legacy group. I aim to draw parallels between the experiences of the FLG members who transformed and those of Malcolm X during a similar period in his life, with a focus on the teachings of traditional/Sunni Islam and its impact on his personal growth.

In chapter 4, I explore leadership within the Black Baptist church and develop a behavioral approach that aligns with their faith context and promotes a social ethic. The goal is to offer valuable insights to leaders within the church about the importance of maintaining a faith disposition that can guide FLG members through transformation. Our faith context must be lived out in ways that can help transform FLG members, especially given the layers of trauma that exist due to the social conditions of black bodies. Therefore, leaders must exhibit a lived behavioral context that aligns with their faith understanding and aids in preventing survival mode relapse. To illustrate this point further, we will analyze the human behaviors of white and non-white Sunni Muslims in Jeddah and Mecca. This analysis will demonstrate how aligning human behaviors with a faith context can alter individuals' perceptions of leadership, the church, and themselves.

In chapter 5, I examine the concepts of Lent and its principles of sacrifice, death, and rebirth, which can act as a catalyst for transformation. I introduce the idea of pilgrimage, which can serve as an active vehicle for the collective congregation to use as a transformation exercise. We will explore topics such as journeying, ritual practice, creating a safe space, and building a community, which can serve as essential tools to redevelop the thought processes and behavioral patterns of FLG members. Lent and pilgrimage will be the "bridging" stage in the transformation process. Once this bridge is created, the congregation and community can develop a new fundamental belief, which can be actualized through modified behavior that transforms the congregation.

In chapter 6, I delve into the effects of transformation on Malcolm and the reformed family legacy group members. I explore the concept of detachment and how it plays a pivotal role

INTRODUCTION

in creating the necessary conduit for transformation. Additionally, I delve into the contrasting experiences of Malcolm and the reformed FLG members as they grapple with the realities of their social context upon returning from pilgrimage. Finally, I examine how personal character traits can either aid or hinder the ability of reformed family group members to confront or retreat from congregational issues that prevent the introduction or reinstitution of established governance, polity, and practices at the Wayside Baptist Church.

In chapter 7, I examine the effects of transformation on individuals who have reformed from a family legacy group and explore the resulting social dynamics within the congregation. This look will compare these transformed individuals and Malcolm X during his pilgrimage period. Furthermore, I will demonstrate how a created congregational culture interpreted as oppositional to new leadership and its aligned ethical stance can be altered, leading to a mutual understanding between FLG members and the leadership within the Black Baptist church.

In this book, I make comparisons between the flawed/distorted teachings of the Honorable Elijah Muhammad and the traditional view of Islam known as Sunni Islam. This comparison offers similarities between an established polity and practices of the Black Baptist church with a contrasting created congregational system or survival modality that I address. To reintroduce this terminology, I assess this created system as "patterned clusters of normatively imbued ideas and concepts, including particular representations of power relations. These conceptual maps help people navigate the complexity of their political universe and carry claims to social truth."[3] The issue with the conduct of the family legacy group lies not in its inconsistency with their means of survival but in its adherence to a belief system and its aligned social behavior, rooted in emotion rather than facts and not based on a traditional religious context. This observation applies to FLGs within the Black Baptist church and the Nation of Islam.

---

3. James, *Ideologies of Globalism*, xii.

INTRODUCTION

While Malcolm X was practicing in the Muslim tradition, and I am offering a transformation model for Christians, my goal is not to attempt to inform Christianity from an Islamic theological lens. Instead, I aim to view the lived experiences and encounters of Malcolm X to critique the tensions and conflicts that exist in the Black Baptist church between family legacy groups and their resistance to a reemergence of an established system of polity and practice. Malcolm X's transformation movement provides a model of what is needed, what needs to happen, and what can and sometimes does happen to address the congregational conflicts formed by the new power culture of FLG members and their aligned ethic, antithetical to the established understanding of belief and behavior in the Black Baptist church.

Although informing Christianity through an Islamic lens is not wrong, I do not seek to wrestle with this perspective in this book. Albeit interfaith dialogue is not the tenor and tone of this book, my premise does not mean to suggest that Christian–Islamic dialogue is wrong or that Christians have nothing to learn from their Muslim neighbors. I ground my perspective in interpreting the second letter to Timothy: "All scripture is inspired by God and is useful for teaching, for reproof, for correction, and training in righteousness."[4] My understanding of the term "all" does not limit God's act of scriptural inspiration to my canon. As a matter of principle, I am clarifying my stance for this book in the particular theological context of the Black church, that the topic/content of my work will not be Christian–Muslim dialogue on theological issues.

While the information in this book is thought-provoking in its presentation, the content does not seek to demean Christianity and elevate Islam. Instead, I speak to the specific elements of personal transformation concerning the structures involved in critically examining power dynamics and social cultures that shape identity and the social behaviors that can be similar across differing religious, cultural, and ethical contexts. This framing synthesizes my thoughts in ways that translate Malcolm X's experiences

4. 2 Tim 3:16.

INTRODUCTION

into an easily approachable, valuable perspective in a congregational/social setting in ways that do not superimpose Islamic views or practices. Thus, while referencing the Black Baptist church, my conclusions based on my content are not limited to Black Baptist churches exclusively.

CHAPTER 1

The Formation of Survival Modalities

LET'S START THIS CHAPTER by understanding the term "survival modalities." This will serve as a mental anchor throughout the book. To define this compound phrase, we'll examine each word separately and combine them into a unified concept. "Survival" denotes persisting in life or existence, often in the face of adversity or hardship. "Modality" refers to a specific way something is experienced or manifested. Therefore, we can define Survival Modalities as the adopted lifestyle patterns of individuals who have faced challenging circumstances. The term itself doesn't imply any positive connotations beyond an individual's determination to endure social, communal, financial, and racial obstacles. Consequently, the need for survival inherently suggests the presence of a preceding difficult situation.

As a result of unforeseen circumstances, higher-order cognitive functions may be temporarily compromised, potentially leading to rash or instinctual actions. Survival modalities can also trigger intense emotional responses, including fear, anxiety, and a feeling of urgency. These emotions serve an adaptive purpose in the short term, motivating individuals to take quick action for self-preservation. The survival mode is a reactive response to social changes in all communal spaces. These dynamics are experienced by individuals who often associate these dynamics with the body's "fight or flight" response, an automatic reaction to perceived danger.[1] When faced with a stressful or threatening situation, the human body initiates certain responses. Individuals experience heightened sensory awareness, becoming more attuned to their environment. This increased alertness enables quick identification and response to potential dangers. The person's focus narrows, concentrating primarily on the perceived threat or stressor, often disregarding other stimuli. In such situations, the brain prioritizes swift decision-making and action over careful deliberation. Whether subtle or pronounced, shifts in social norms affect the emotional states of those involved in these spaces, particularly when the causes of these changes are unexpected or rooted in social tension. Although psychological, the concept of survival modalities has implications for Black religious organizations.

SURVIVAL MODE EXISTENCE IN BLACK RELIGIOUS SPACES

Our interpretation of difficult situations does not begin with our referenced congregation but rather with Black communities and religious organizations in America. Assessing the history of Blacks and Black communities in America through the lens of social difficulty is self-explanatory. While I am aware that our history and even our future appears challenged, I do not wish to take a deep dive on the matter at this point in the book. In looking at the historical framing of a few Black religious movements in America, it is safe to imply that social and religious tensions not only contributed to the formation of these movements but also the development of what I describe as survival modalities. Although the effects of racialization and trauma for Black bodies are not universal, I wish to offer context to my claim by providing an abridged historical description of three Black religious organizations in America: the AME Church, the Nation of Islam (NOI), and the Black Baptist denominational conventions.

1. Cleveland Clinic, "Fight, Flight, Freeze, or Fawn?"

The Formation of Survival Modalities

For the African Methodist Episcopal Church, due to racial discrimination, Pastor Richard Allen, Absalom Jones, and others established Bethel in Philadelphia in 1787. To establish Bethel's independence from interfering white Methodists, Allen successfully pressed charges in the Pennsylvania courts in 1807 and 1815 for the right of his congregation to exist as an independent institution. As a result, other Black Methodists seeking autonomy connected themselves with Allen and formed the African American Episcopal denomination.[2]

For the Americanized Muslim Movement founded in 1930, known as the Nation of Islam, Elijah Muhammad, successor of Wallace D. Fard Muhammad, grounded his teachings to his followers in the NOI on the philosophy of Noble Drew Ali. Noble Drew Ali grounded his philosophy not on the traditional ways or understandings of Old World Islam but on Moorish identity.[3] Thus, his philosophy emphasized Black identity, experience, and the superiority of the Black man over any other race. Elijah Muhammad not only "took this idea and placed it at the center of his understanding of Islam but adopted Drew Ali's particularistic formula for understanding Islam and turned it into the most well-known tradition in the history of African American Islam."[4]

Adverse tensions amongst Black and white citizens in America facilitated the dynamics of hate for whites into the minds of most, if not all, of Elijah Muhammad's followers. Even if there was room to reframe this philosophy into one that created unification between whites and Black people as expressed in the traditional teachings of Old World Islam, American racism, sociopolitical prejudice, and the social construct of whiteness in America nullified any hopes of contributing to a new way of living together. This premise laid the foundation for the formation of NOI's survival modality.

For the Black Baptist denominational movement, the origins of the Black Baptist movement are not traced easily. Enslaved

---

2. Dickerson, "Our History."
3. Curtis, *Islam in Black America*, 85.
4. Curtis, *Islam in Black America*, 85.

Black Baptists worshiped on plantations under the supervision of white preachers as early as the 1750s. However, independent Black Baptist congregations did not emerge until just before the War for Independence.[5] Social and conventional division was not the result of the social construct of whiteness primarily but rather matters of position relating to publication ownership, social and political differences, and theological distinctions. As a result of these reasons, we now have a splintered list of Black Baptist religious organizations in America: the National Baptist Convention of America; the National Baptist Convention, USA; Lott Carey Foreign Mission; Progressive Baptist National Convention; American Baptist Missionary Convention; the National Primitive Baptist Convention; and the Full Gospel Baptist Church Fellowship.

Similarly, local Black Baptist congregations have experienced challenges due to congregational splits and splintering, leaving Black churches left to create a modality needful for existence and survival. This premise grounds the social and congregational experiences of our referenced congregation. Reflecting on the Wayside Baptist Church, Wayside formed itself because of tensions in their previous religious affiliation. As a result of a congregational split, Wayside formed a new church but never healed from the effects of previous congregational challenges. While departing from their former church separated them from what some view as a troubled congregation, we learned through their lived experiences with church difficulties that congregational tensions were deeply ingrained in the fabric of their culture. Thus, leaving did not produce liberation. Instead, they carried with them to their new church the same social dispositions they already embodied. While social tensions historically birthed most of our predominately Black religious organizations in America, survival modalities in certain spaces may not be the result of racial discrimination only but also irreconcilable congregational differences.

---

5. Dixie, "Black Baptists."

The Formation of Survival Modalities

SURVIVAL MODALITIES IN THE BLACK BAPTIST CHURCH

In offering a brief synopsis of what contributes to forming survival modalities in religious organizations, how, then, do we associate our understanding of survival modalities with trauma-based occurrences in the Black church? Investigating survival modalities in the context of the Black church posits varying outcomes in our current cultural, congregational, and social context compared to the Black church in the 1960s. Historically, the Black community's unique historical, social, and cultural experiences shaped the church and its members' responses to adversity. Religious participation significantly impacted how individuals coped with social stressors and shaped their lifestyles. Religious practices sought to reduce exposure to stressors and promote a sense of calm among members. Additionally, religious communities provided opportunities for forming friendships and engaging in shared social activities with like-minded individuals. These communities fostered access to support networks and enhanced the perception of their reliability. How then does a congregation function when unforeseen occurrences cause negative social dispositions to resurface within church culture?

While not all Black Baptist churches subscribe to my theory, several Black Baptist churches are personality-driven. Thus, the absence of a pastoral figure associates itself with an unforeseen occurrence and affects the complexion of the congregation. Typically, this transition leads to shifts in congregation dynamics, economic downturn, and a lack of community impact. What are we going to do, and how will we move forward? These are the frequent questions that come to mind. Exemplary references to pastorless Black Baptist churches are often framed as uncertain. While the established system and culture of the Black Baptist church is not thrown away, some variables at work do not allow the trauma-based remnants to function as usual. Perception in this congregational/social context produces trauma, and trauma moves those who remain to operate in a new way: survival.

When No One Leads the Church

Let us look at Wayside as an example to clarify this collective association. Reverend Right has pastored the Wayside Baptist Church for twenty-five years. Reverend Right provided weekly messages to the congregation, and the membership functioned in a pastor-led style of structure and practice. Wayside underwent a typical three-stage progression that most Black Baptist churches experience. This progression is commonly referred to as the form, the storm, and the norm. Initially, there is often a sense of formality as the new congregational leader assumes their role. Subsequently, conflicts may arise regarding personality, leadership decisions, and ministry choices, creating storms for the leadership and the congregation. Once these issues are resolved, a new congregational norm emerges. As year twenty-five neared its completion, Rev. Right decided that his time as Wayside's pastor had reached its climax. An announcement that Rev. Right was transitioning from the church unsettled the congregation. Although several members stood up and clapped to support his decision, most congregants displayed signs of fear, frustration, and sadness at the news. What will the church do after Rev. Right leaves? Who will impact and inform its functionality now?

In this context, survival modalities function in two specific ways. For the congregant, they work as an emotional, physical, and psychological reaction to transient leadership. To the remaining leadership dynamic in the church, survival modalities exist as tools that develop the internal fortitude necessary for navigating adversity and fostering what some would consider a spirit of perseverance. Although the conditions associated with the church are tense and uncertain, leaders and family groups must continue to provide a social narrative that presents the church as a sanctuary for all, a space for healing, and a catalyst for social change, no matter how unique their congregational context fluctuates.

The departure or retirement of a long-serving pastor can profoundly impact a church like Wayside. Pastors serve as constant pillars of community leadership, support, guidance, and mentorship. From the pastor's perspective, it may be a time of change or well-deserved rest after years of service, but from the congregation's perspective, it is a time of loss. Additionally, many churches, including Wayside, do not have a clear succession plan for leadership roles. This is particularly true for pastoral positions. While one of many, this example provides a surface overview of an impactful transition in Black Baptist churches and the effects of congregational perceptions and traumas based on their congregational/social context and culture. While my premise is not exclusive to all Black Baptist churches, it does fit the description of several urban Black Baptist congregations of similar context and culture.

In similar Black Baptist churches, the absence of a structured succession plan often leads to disruptions within the church, causing specific ministries to falter due to a lack of leadership continuity. In such situations, other individuals in the church may step up to provide guidance and support. Still, tensions can arise if their advice conflicts with the ambitions of those seeking power and influence during this vulnerable period for the church. Despite efforts to maintain stability, those assuming leadership roles must grapple with the realities of their new positions, which may be more challenging than anticipated. My working example connects the emotional responses displayed by the congregants with descriptions of unforeseen circumstances that altered the members' perceptions in the congregational setting. The alteration of perception without clarity of understanding produced trauma. Thus, perception contributes to the development of trauma, and trauma, in association with perception, impacts the emotional disposition in individuals and groups that foster survival modalities.

THE CHALLENGES WITH SUSTAINED SURVIVAL MODALITIES

While survival modalities are a natural and adaptive response to immediate challenges, their lifespan should be temporal. Survival modalities should never exist as a new normal in religious/social spaces. Instead, it should serve as a balm that aids an immediate crisis. Renowned philosophy and cognitive science professor

Susanna Schellenberg asserts that "perception grounds demonstrative reference, yields singular thoughts, and fixes the reference of singular terms. Moreover, perception provides us with knowledge on particulars in our environment and justifies singular thoughts about particulars."[6] Schellenberg explores the relationship between how we perceive, refer to, and understand things, particularly in the context of philosophy of mind, language, and behavior. She proposes that our perceptual abilities are fundamental to using demonstrative expressions to point out objects in our surroundings. Our direct sensory experiences of the world, enabled by perception, provide the groundwork for demonstrative reference.

Additionally, perception not only aids in reference but also allows for the creation of singular thoughts grounded in specific contexts. The passage only raises concerns if our perceptions appear flawed or inaccurate. In that case, perception might impact the validity of singular thoughts and potentially affect their justification. Here is our challenge with perception through a trauma-based lens.

When perception grounds our mode and exists as a congregational/social fixture beyond its needfulness, it impacts the power dynamics and the congregational/social identity. Modalities meant to foster stability during moments of transition now exist as the status quo. Additionally, the ethics aligned with this new status quo appear opposing to the established system and practices where they exist. Ronald W. Richardson, in *Creating a Healthier Church*, asks, "What is it about human nature, about our strengths and liabilities as people, and about the way we organize ourselves in groups that make things go well or poorly when we are faced with problems?"[7] Richardson explores the ways individuals and groups address challenges and how the inherent qualities and limitations of human nature significantly influence those challenges. Our positive attributes, such as inventiveness, adaptability, compassion, and collaborative spirit, enable us to confront difficulties, adjust to new situations, and devise creative solutions. Nevertheless, our

6. Schellenberg, "Perceptual Particularity," 25.
7. Richardson, *Creating a Healthier Church*, 20.

shortcomings, including anxiety, prejudice, self-centeredness, and ineffective communication, can result in disagreements, passivity, or less-than-ideal results.

The formation of groups can either enhance or diminish these characteristics. When people collaborate with well-defined objectives, confidence in one another, and mutual admiration, they can surmount considerable hurdles. Conversely, if groups lack organization, trust, or unity, problems may escalate and progress becomes more challenging. In the end, the interplay between human strengths and weaknesses, coupled with the dynamics of group unity and guidance, determines our effectiveness in navigating challenges. From this viewpoint, how should we interpret perceptions and their effects in a religious/social arena? Furthermore, what criteria should we use to determine what is effective and what is not? Whose perspective should serve as our standard for evaluation?

In the following example, let me reference one of my experiences as a newly elected leader of a particular Black Baptist church. In my specific case, I belonged to the lineage of passing pulpiteers. I was not a constant fixture; I was another pulpit pilgrim who graced the church but never transitioned from student visa to permanent resident. One of the board members informed me that the church did not know what they were doing. Little did I know that implementing Scripture and adhering to the tenets of their constitution and bylaws as a means of congregational development disrupted their church functioning. While members of the dominant power group were not opposed to the Bible per se, there were moments of mild frustration when topics centered around methodology (how we do things) and rationale (why we do things) were discussed. During those moments, my biblical interpretation(s) and calls to action were disregarded because they did not advocate the "do it how I want it done or do it the way we have always done it" methodology of the family legacy group (FLG) in the Black Baptist church where I served.

Because I was an outsider in their space, my words were embraced only by those new to the church and those who associated themselves with the church's established/traditional governing system, not those who were a part of the dominant power group in the church. Their system, one based on perception and trauma, exercised in the congregational arena beyond a moment of temporal needfulness, became embedded in the religious and cultural practices of the church over time.

While my example is exclusive to a particular congregational experience, can you imagine the impact of a sustained survival modality within a congregational setting that undergoes many pastoral transitions throughout the church? Can you envision a church that opts to remain in a perpetual state of survival modality because the reality of transitional leadership is the only dynamic that is consistent in their congregational/social context?

In assessing my personal ministry experience comparable to the experiences of the Wayside Baptist Church, I discovered that a sustained survival modality served as the congregation's identity marker. Their current governance and practice tools represent who they are, not who they were. The challenges associated with the reintegration of their standard constitution, bylaws, and Bible-based suggestions seem problematic based on the workability of that which is in place. While FLG members serve as the voices of influence and power within the congregational space, the social/congregational identity markers do not reflect a sense of collective mutuality or interdependency but rather an identity informed by the group who assumed power and control, who continued in like fashion by sustaining a sole dependency model in the church. One could suggest that prolonged survival modalities only exist as an issue to those who do not define or control the power dynamic in the congregation. How do we postulate that this sustained modality is perceived as opposing when the church functions? These thoughts rest on the opposite sides of the congregational pendulum of interpreting the impacts of perception, governance, and practices appropriate in the congregational/social space.

The Formation of Survival Modalities

THE INTERSECTIONALITY OF MALCOLM X AND THE FLG ON SURVIVAL MODALITIES

To assess the connections between Malcolm X's pre-hajj experiences and encounters with individuals who subscribe to the sustainability of survival modalities in the Black Baptist church, I must offer a brief historical look at Malcolm's formation and its association with the religious culture and modality of the Americanized Black Muslim Movement, also known as the Nation of Islam. In terms of interpretation, my connection to Malcolm's experiences and those of Black Baptist church members shows parallels rooted in shared social encounters. As such, I will provide examples for these common social experiences without promoting the adoption of Islamic theological beliefs or practices among those within a Christian framework.

Although the socioeconomic/sociopolitical impacts of Americanized racism contributed to Malcolm's perception and social trauma, the philosophy of Marcus Garvey during his formative years and the teachings of the Honorable Elijah Muhammad during his adult years served as a counterweight to the social construct of whiteness in America. The social construct in America is a representation of what I previously asserted as a difficult situation relating to the Black Baptist Church. Black Nationalism was a central building block of Malcolm's understanding of Black life and identity before his association with the Nation of Islam. Malcolm X, formally known as Malcolm Little, was the fourth son of two followers of Marcus Garvey, Earl and Louise Little. Marcus Garvey, founder of the Universal Negro Improvement Association (UNIA) in 1914, stressed racial pride and self-improvement.[8] Garvey believed that white society would never accept Black Americans as equals. Therefore, he called for the separate self-development of African Americans within the United States. As followers of the philosophy and ideals taught by Marcus Garvey, Earl and Louise instilled Marcus Garvey's philosophies into the lives of their children and the Black people within their communities.

---

8. Dagnini, "Marcus Garvey," 199.

According to Les and Tamara Payne in *The Dead Are Arising: The Life of Malcolm X,*

> As for the parents of young Malcolm, pride in Africa aside, they clung to the essence of Garvey's message, even after his deportation, rejecting the racial submissiveness so widespread among Negroes. With self-assurance and a sense of equanimity, Earl and Louise Little steadfastly worked to instill in their children a key Garvey credo: Liberate the minds of men, and ultimately, you will liberate the bodies of men.[9]

Thus, Malcolm's founding understanding of self-assurance, identity, and separation from whiteness lived long before his association with the Nation of Islam (NOI). What can be understood about his upbringing is the connectedness of what his parents taught him and what he would eventually live out as a representative of the Nation of Islam. This correlation between the two was not a newfound revelation but a reintroduction to a formerly taught ideal that laid the foundation for his understanding of value and significance as a Black man in America. Malcolm would use black nationalism as the vehicle to drive his social justice agenda. Black nationalism would inevitably exist as the cover and bookend of Malcolm's life. Before he was introduced to Allah, he was introduced to Garveyism. Thus, what he developed within him as an adolescent would emerge in his adulthood and ground his sociopolitical agenda.

At the core of this connection between his adolescent and adult life rests his experiences and encounters with whiteness. Whether "being taunted by racial abuse throughout his childhood, haunted by his father's tragic end, or ambivalent about how it occurred,"[10] Malcolm had a history of experiences and encounters with whites that represented the racial tensions common in mid-century America. Whether Jim Crow or the KKK, whether in Omaha, Lansing, East Lansing, Detroit, Boston, or even Harlem, USA, racial tensions were a permanent fixture in Malcolm's

---

9. Payne, *Dead Are Arising*, loc. 54.
10. DeCaro, *On the Side*, loc. 30.

life from birth until he was no more. Thus, racialization by way of housing, social prejudice, vocational aspirations, and judicial bias all contributed to his social perception and developed traumas.

While these occurrences in Malcolm's life date back fifty to one hundred years, Black people in America still encounter tensions centered around racialization in housing discrimination and restrictions, limited job opportunities, judicial bias, racial profiling, biased policing, stymied sociopolitical engagement, and challenges to educational equity. Horowitz, Brown, and Cox, of the Pew Research Center, offer context to this claim in their article entitled "Views of Racial Inequality." They posit the following: "More than four-in-ten Americans say the country still has work to do to give black people equal rights with whites. Blacks, in particular, are skeptical that black people will ever have equal rights in this country."[11] This statement highlights a significant and ongoing racial divide in American views on progress toward racial equality in the United States. Although many Americans recognize that the country has not yet achieved complete equality between Black and White citizens, there is a concerning level of doubt, particularly among Black Americans, about whether genuine equality will ever be attained. This reflects both an understanding of the work that remains and fatigue stemming from centuries of unmet promises and systemic injustices.

This further compels us to address the disparity between recognizing issues and taking action to address them. Acknowledging that the nation still has progress to make is merely the initial step; the more challenging endeavor is reforming the systems that sustain inequality. Black skepticism stems not from cynicism but from lived experiences—a historical understanding that advancements in America often occur inconsistently and under certain conditions. The call to action involves two main objectives: First, we need to strive for a society that progresses beyond mere symbolic actions to achieve substantial and systemic reforms in areas such as education, housing, law enforcement, and the economy. Second, for the African American community, it is essential to

---

11. Horowitz, "Views of Racial Inequality," 1.

continue fostering networks of resilience, advocacy, and faith that not only confront injustice but also envision a future where equality is actively practiced, not just promised. Genuine equality relies not only on laws or public sentiment but also on the nation's moral resolve to confront its history and envision a new future.

This reality sets the background for the teaching philosophy of Elijah Muhammad. While Elijah's teachings were antithetical to traditional Sunni Islamic views and traditions, the Nation of Islam's lived-out perceptions, better known as their socioreligious ethics, were intriguing to Malcolm. To Malcolm X's declaration,

> I never had seen any Christian-believing Negros conduct themselves like the Muslims, the individuals, and the families alike. I had never dreamed of anything like that atmosphere among Black people who had learned to be proud they were Black, who had learned to love other Black people instead of being jealous and suspicious.[12]

For Malcolm X, the principles and practices of Islam, as lived out by the Nation of Islam, presented no appearances of fault, at least to present and prospective members. What was witnessed was the pushback against racism and the Nation's stance against the denigration of the Black individual. What mattered in this socioreligious space during the 1960s was how Black bodies developed a collective support mechanism. This mechanism reshaped how they saw and thought about themselves in contrast to the hierarchical interpretation of Black identity created by the social construct of whiteness in America. This grounds my thoughts on how the NOI was viewed by those outside of the Nation, not as a religious sect in the universal sense only but as a Black nationalist group, existing under the banner of a religious group, seeking to liberate and empower Black people from the chains of oppression in America.

---

12. Malcolm X, *Autobiography of Malcolm X*, 198–99.

The Formation of Survival Modalities
SURVIVAL MODALITIES AS A MAINTAINED SYSTEM OF EXISTENCE

For Malcolm X, Black identity and social/cultural/economic awareness rested at his core. In assessing the social trauma of whiteness to how white identity juxtaposed with Black identity, self-appreciation and self-worth for followers of the Nation of Islam were paramount above traditional religious correctness. Thus, traditional Quranic interpretation and practice, not taught by Elijah Muhammad or practiced fully by the members of the NOI, did not serve as the call for an association with the Nation of Islam—social conduct did.

Although spoken statements against governmental systems in America and religious differences between the Nation of Islam and several religious organizations, including Sunni Muslims, posited Malcolm X and the nation as oppositional, one cannot nullify the impact, the perceptions, or the traumas experienced by Black people based on the social construct in America. Blacks have always lived in a perpetual state of survival mode in America. While their reality has sometimes been falsely assessed and incorrectly diagnosed, some social/religious modalities and aligned ethics are a byproduct of social conditioning. Let us look at a few of Malcolm X's experiences and encounters that reflect this notion shared with the Public Broadcasting System.

In 1928, as an adolescent, Malcolm's family moved into a predominantly white area in Michigan. Due to zoning restrictions, his family was sued and evicted because they were not white. In 1939, after the murder of his father, he and his siblings were placed in different foster homes. Even though Malcolm excelled in school, he was discouraged from pursuing a dream of becoming a lawyer. In 1946, while tried and convicted for grand larceny with an accomplice, two white women had their sentences vacated while Malcolm served ten years in prison.[13]

For Malcolm, the tenets of social conditioning were Americanized racism. Racism was present in his formative years and

---

13. PBS, "Timeline of Malcolm X's Life."

his adult years. Malcolm could not become a conformist to the traditional system of America because that system was antithetical to his existence as a Black man. Thus, it was essential that he not only embraced a survival modality but empowered other Blacks in America to embrace it. Although the survival mode dynamic of the Nation of Islam was impactful to Blacks relating to the social construct in America, it remained in opposition to a traditional Sunni Islamic belief and practice.

While racism in America impacts the Black community in general, racism as a social construct does not serve as a conduit or source to the internal perceptions and traumas associated with the development of survival modalities in most of our current urban-based Black churches. The need for survival modalities in specific congregational/social spaces may be essential to our understanding.

One specific challenge with challenging a sustained modality and attempting to reintegrate an established system of functionality is that it poses no issues to those who comprise the congregational/social space. Most members are not aware of either purpose or intent within the congregational/social context. As social dilemmas present themselves and actions are taken by the leadership structure to rectify the issues, what curbs the masses are the results, not necessarily the rules or modality used. Thus, the pushback to the nullification of survival modalities and the reintegration of an established system does not impact the body in the same way it affects the leader or body who understands its need and usefulness to the greater working mission.

OUR OUTCOME REGARDING SURVIVAL MODALITIES

The question at the intersection of survival modalities and traditional systems is this: in what ways does moral deliberation factor into the equation? While general in its inquisition, I am discovering that the premise of moral rightness is subjective. Since social and congregational arenas, including Black Baptist churches, are democratic regarding decision-making, does congregational democracy help or hinder the practices and culture of the church? J. J. Tillman asserts that "democracy complicates things."[14] He further states,

> Within quite broad social limits, this effectively allows each person to determine what he or she accepts as the morally right thing, and so democracies have become societies filled with moral authorities, all who believe their personal moral values are the right ones.[15]

Relating to my reference congregation, sustained survival modalities may be useful during moments of transient leadership. While I have interpreted its presence from the lens of shaped congregational culture and power dynamics, considering its ability to offer somewhat sustenance, survival modalities in periods of pastoral transition have moral value for some. First, let us assess the congregational space through the lens of morality. Suppose morality is a system of beliefs or values relating to proper conduct against which behavior is considered acceptable or unacceptable. How do the remaining congregants assess what is right if members do not practice critical thinking? Furthermore, suppose the created system that aids them in moments of trauma and transition is the byproduct of the newly influential voices in the church. How do we determine that their system is seemingly wrong if it is the system that is sustaining the ministry?

Suppose congregations are neither obstacles to the reconstruction of coherent moral opinions nor the passive recipients of already worked-out answers but a place where ethical reflection, formulation, and action occur. Can survival modalities provide ethical validity in their belief and behavior in ways that are beneficial to the whole, even if it is perceived as opposing to a traditional/established way? While they can, the challenge is that survival modalities at their core are the byproduct of negatively induced tensions and trauma-based reactions. While the ability to make the

---

14. Tillman, *Integrative Model*, 2.
15. Tillman, *Integrative Model*, 2.

best of a trauma-based scenario is plausible, fundamentally, these modalities void the opportunity to expand themselves beyond the reality of an existence that does not oppose. Does survival have to exist as a congregation's only means of functionality? Can the notion of thriving be an option? If so, how do we transition from the theory of flourishing to the implementation of thriving in congregational/social spaces?

CHAPTER 2

Social Origins of Family Legacy Group Members

Exploring the idea of origin reveals the elements that have influenced our current state. In social and communal settings, it becomes clear that power dynamics play a vital role in our social foundations. The way power is distributed ultimately influences the direction of religious or community systems. However, the quest for power can sometimes overshadow the community's values and norms, potentially causing an imbalance in the power structure. This scenario can create the impression that power is relatively easy to acquire in such settings, highlighting the possible consequences of this issue. It is crucial to acknowledge and address this matter, as it can have significant implications for communities.

Congregational societies form the foundation of every church's structure. Within each congregation, there exists a group or groups of individuals who wield significant influence within the church community, both overtly and subtly. These individuals can deeply impact others in the church, who may either follow their lead or provide crucial financial support to the congregation. In times of change, this group can emerge as critical problem-solvers or serve as trusted advisors to the congregation, thereby demonstrating their pivotal role in the church's evolution. This group, known as the "family legacy group," or "power group" for clarity, holds a substantial and significant influence in the church community, a fact that cannot be overstated. Their influence is not just a matter of power but also a matter of shaping the very culture of the congregational community.

Exploring the social origins of power groups interpreted as family legacy groups requires an examination of the historical and social context in which they exist. My evaluation will seek to identify the effects of educational disparity, challenges associated with identity formation, social conditioning, social trauma, and family systems as contributing factors to their social origins. I believe that trauma grounds their formation and thus has negatively impacted how FLG members see themselves and socially/congregationally engage with individuals who have a different world/congregational view.

EDUCATION DISPARITY AS A CONSIDERING FACTOR

For more than a century, New Jersey has been characterized by a divide concerning educational equality and equity. In a 2013 article titled, "A Tale of Two Deeply Divided NJ Public School Systems," author Paul L. Tractenberg states, "The state is home to one school system that is urban and populated by poor students of color; another, suburban and populated by well-to-do white students."[1] Urban school systems have faced disparities in access to quality education for over a century. Even though segregation is no longer legal, New Jersey continues to be one of the most racially divided states in terms of education. Black students frequently find themselves in schools where most of their classmates come from low-income backgrounds, which restricts their access to academic opportunities.

Urban districts with mostly Black students often receive less financial support per student than wealthier, predominantly white suburban areas. Schools in economically disadvantaged Black neighborhoods typically offer fewer Advanced Placement

1. Tractenberg, "Tale of Two," 1.

or honors courses, which contributes to achievement gaps and hinders college preparedness. High rates of teacher turnover in these underfunded districts disrupt the continuity of education and student support. In New Jersey, Black students are more likely to be suspended or expelled, which can lead them into the school-to-prison pipeline.

Poor educational outcomes make it more challenging for Black youth to pursue higher education and secure stable, well-paying jobs, thereby perpetuating cycles of intergenerational poverty. Students in schools with limited resources may internalize low academic expectations, affecting their self-esteem and long-term goals. Curricula that lack cultural representation and relevance can alienate Black students and reduce their engagement. Urban school systems in New Jersey have faced disparities in access to quality education for over a century due to systemic racism, social classism, and insufficient financial and resource support.

IDENTITY FORMATION AS A CONSIDERING FACTOR

Depending on the salience of Black culture in their growing-up experience, Black cultural messages influence Black identity development.[2] Consider the potential effects on Black identity if the cultural message diminishes in prominence. How might societal factors such as economic and educational disparities within the Black community shape this identity? Furthermore, suppose Black individuals ground their identity in misinformation, social disorder, and congregational misplacement. How might we evaluate their mental, spiritual, and emotional perspectives within the context of the Black church? To better understand the historical context of the community where most Wayside Baptist Church members either grew up or currently reside, it is essential to highlight the urban area's social landscape.

2. Wijeyesinghe, *New Perspectives*, 41.

When No One Leads the Church

Upon analyzing the social dynamics of the Wayside Baptist Church, its congregation and community, I discovered numerous members share familial ties and have a long-standing history of residing near one another. This close-knit atmosphere intensifies the effects of collective sharing, whether positive or negative, due to their frequent social interactions. The Wayside Baptist Church serves as both a religious and community hub for its members, who must navigate the constantly evolving leadership and ongoing social challenges the Black community encounters in America.

Consider this: suppose members of a family legacy group exhibit behaviors that seem at odds to a new congregational leader or members of the congregation who have varying perspectives concerning organizational functioning. How should we assess their actions? Furthermore, how should our understanding be if these behaviors are an integral part of their identity? Are such actions essential for them to feel a sense of presence or to maintain their limited existence in the world, even if they are perceived as oppositional?

As a minority within a minority, the church is often the only space available for some individuals to uphold and express their identity. If this forms the foundation of their beliefs, how do we interpret how they function and operate when their ultimate purpose is to preserve their identity? Could push back against change be a byproduct of fear? Perhaps their perspective suggests that new or returning governance could minimize their identity. In this light, if we view their resistance as confrontation, could we potentially miss their fight's more profound meaning and purpose? While my congregational experience does not subscribe to a created ideology as an interpretation of identity sustainability, there may be scenarios where this theory may have validity. My experience as a congregational leader understands that all groups have an origin story. Some congregations have had their share of good and troublesome experiences. The question is this: in what ways can the family legacy group see themselves in a new way?

SOCIAL CONDITIONING AS A CONSIDERING FACTOR

When studying the factors influencing social behaviors, we easily overlook a crucial truth in our hypothesis: various socializing agents shape individuals daily. These agents, including family, community, faith-based institutions, schools, and social clubs, carry the distinct aspects of Black/African American culture and inform our overall understanding. It is imperative to recognize the impact of these institutions when investigating the development of social behaviors. When considering this topic, it is essential to consider multiple factors. Firstly, power dynamics must be acknowledged. In Black family structures, the matriarch or patriarch holds significant power, often serving as the voice of reason and understanding. Secondly, extended family members have positions of influence and impact each other based on their socialization, peer relations, and social status.

In terms of the community, it serves as a platform for reinforcing both positive and negative behaviors through socialization. When individuals assess the context of their community and the institutions that socialize them, they tend to adopt the opinions and advice of those who embody the lifestyle they aspire to have. This is based on the belief that following these guidelines will lead to a similar outcome. As a result, people tend to follow and listen to those who hold power and influence within their social circles. The social origins of FLG members, influenced by these entities, shape their perceptions and mindsets in contrast to the established system of polity and practice that we will explore later in this book.

To understand the social origins of FLG members, examining the complex social and relational dynamics that influence their self-perception and community involvement is necessary. The family legacy group's members are also affected by the social conditions where they serve. Members of the family legacy group are not implants. Most are residents of the community. Even those who have moved to other areas still have family ties in the community. Thus, they remain impacted by the same socioeconomic challenges, education disparities, and discriminative practices that plague Black families in that area. As such, the church is not merely a gathering space but an extension of their social/family association. This premise suggests that the family not only attends the church but frames the organizational practices of the church.

If a church displays a selective or biased perception of correctness based on its self-evaluation, some suggests it functions as a family-run church. Although nothing is wrong with connecting to a family-integrated congregation, when trauma exists as a core component of its formation, there are adverse issues that surface throughout its existence. These issues materialize in the form of congregational behaviors that ultimately impact those in the church who are not members of the family legacy group. As previously stated, the core group that started Wayside Baptist Church left Highway to Heaven Baptist Church over congregational issues. In launching Wayside, they sought to be seen and heard. Together, they have a congregation of their own, a space where they are in control.

Often, the challenge in spaces like this is that they are sometimes void of critical thinkers. While I am not suggesting that individuals with limited knowledge and know-how govern these spaces, I am implying that conversations are seldom had with individuals outside of their purview who offer a varying lens of interpretation and suggestion on governance and organizational functioning. Because the trauma of their past experiences has not been addressed, the church is left to make things up as they go. If someone seeks to associate themselves with the church that embodies talents, skills, and experiences, these individuals who are outsiders are often rejected or dismissed, whether directly or passively. When this happens, the church experiences a continual cycle of membership/leadership shuffling that hinders the ministry from growing beyond the family legacy group in the church. For Eric C. Lincoln and Lawrence H. Mamiya, "the Black Church has often found itself repeating history it has already experienced and relearning lessons it has long since forgotten."[3] While the

---

3. Lincoln, *Black Church*, xii.

Social Origins of Family Legacy Group Members

repetition of historical tensions persists, it is doubtful that any lessons are learned in this congregational context.

What we witness in some Black churches associates itself more with dissonance reduction than a direct association with the American social construct understood as racism. Dissonance reduction refers to

> the process by which a person reduces the uncomfortable psychological state resulting from inconsistency among cognitive system elements. Dissonance can be reduced by making one or more inconsistent elements consistent with other elements in the system, by decreasing the perceived importance of an inconsistent element, or by adding new consistent elements to the system.[4]

While affected by what happened to them, this medium implies that an individual justifies ill-intended behaviors toward others by psychologically reducing either the value of the act administered to others or the value of the individual affected by it. Thus, while it is understood that the social construct of racism impacts Blacks on a few levels, demeaning and demoralizing behaviors administered by Blacks on Blacks are a result of dissonance reduction.

I reflect on the congregational tensions experienced by the core group of family legacy members who transitioned from their congregation of origin before the formation of Wayside Baptist Church. Some of the similar experiences they had in the past have resurfaced. This time, they are the givers instead of the recipients. While several years have passed since the formation of the Wayside Baptist Church, the same psychological dispositions from generations past still exist in the actions and ideologies of present members of the family legacy group. In assessing the social origins of FLG members in Black Baptist churches, several factors significantly impact the development of their ideas, ideals, and social behaviors, which individuals outside their group's social dynamic interpret as oppositional. In this book section, Dr.

---

4. *APA Dictionary of Psychology*, "Dissonance Reduction."

Joy DeGruy Leary, PhD, will serve as a primary conversational resource around trauma.

SOCIAL TRAUMA AS A CONSIDERING FACTOR

Exploring the social origins of FLG members requires a careful examination of trauma as a considering factor that shapes their thoughts and beliefs. Trauma, in various forms, can significantly impact mindset, emotions, beliefs, and behaviors. A historical analysis of FLG members suggests that distress, frustration, and conflict exist as a constant social experience within the congregation. According to Dr. Joy DeGruy Leary, "The impact of trauma can manifest in our actions and beliefs. These behaviors may have once been necessary for survival but can now impede our success."[5] In the case of Wayside Baptist Church, a trauma-based mindset and its associated behaviors have developed as a means of coping during periods of leadership gaps. While newly elected congregational leaders view their social dispositions as oppositional, their created ideologies and aligned behaviors enabled the congregation to survive numerous gap periods without an elected leader, which lasted up to three to five years at a time over the life of the church's existence.

The use of this platform prompts me to ponder an alternative interpretation. While I will delve into the risks of prolonged survival strategies later in this publication, do newly appointed congregational leaders and church boards frequently extend historical transparency to one another? Has a moment existed before tension arises when a conversation provides background to ever-evolving emotional states? Is there space beyond the weekly service for discussions on congregational and societal issues that serve as triggers? How can an open dialogue about the challenges, pitfalls, and hurts from past experiences contribute to a more empathetic social atmosphere?

---

5. Leary, *Post Traumatic Slave Syndrome*, 117.

Social Origins of Family Legacy Group Members

This subject holds great significance for me. People's present emotional and behavioral states are frequently observed, but the underlying reasons are often overlooked. Instead of understanding the roots of their aggressive/passive-aggressive behavior, we tend to categorize individuals as issues based on their reactions to the existing system. Although the family legacy group of the Wayside Baptist Church faced some obstacles, they overcame them by relying on their internal strengths. Their leadership as a focused group and their established system helped stabilize the congregation during times of social and congregational challenge.

While Wayside may not have a stellar reputation, they maintained the church building, church grounds, and a parsonage without a seated congregational leader. While these strategies were effective during transitional periods, they were considered unnecessary after selecting a permanent pastor. The real challenge came when a new leader was selected, and their philosophy of ministry did not align with the system created to maintain the church as it was. My premise speaks to their philosophy, not their preaching style or teaching pedagogy. Often, this understanding rests as the bedrock of challenges between what is and what can be in most congregational/social arenas. Whenever changes are made or even brought up, they serve as a social or emotional trigger. Still, leadership inconsistencies for Wayside made it challenging to let go of an ideology intended to be temporal.

Given their congregation's unexpected and brief leadership moments, members of the family legacy group were compelled to rely on survival tactics. Despite the appearance of a conventional high worship-style service during Sunday gatherings, these tactics were employed in the organization's day-to-day operations rather than during the worship service. While this approach went against established policies and traditions, it eventually became the church's norm due to its leadership's inconsistent nature and functioning. Much like the American social structure, some FLG members of some Black Baptist churches have shown resistance to change. Although open to growth and progress, their willingness to accept alterations only frames themselves within the confines of their current congregational construct.

Let us look to the Nation of Islam's encounters with whites in America during its formative years. By evaluating several events with whites, we get a fresh understanding why W. D. Fard and Elijah Poole, later know as Elijah Muhammad, held to their stance concerning whites. The Nation of Islam's ideology of whites being perceived as devils date back to before Elijah became its longest-tenured leader of the Nation. For W. D. Fard, he knew far too well the social prejudices superimposed on Blacks in Detroit and Chicago. For Elijah Poole, who would later become Elijah Muhammad, he knew far too well the lynchings of Black bodies by white men in the name of white supremacy.

Although faith in Allah was essential to the Black Muslims, their experience with whites in America was too traumatic to ever consider them as brothers, knowing what had been done and even what they were still doing to Blacks across this country. Thus, while perceived as controversial, members of the Nation of Islam must do whatever was necessary to maintain their status quo. This is reminiscent of the experiences of FLG members, who had to rely on their proven sustainability methods over governance of the larger group, which they were not sure would work, let alone be accepted, even to the detriment of congregational peace. While members of the Nation engage in a few religious practices, e.g., daily prayers and fasting, to name a few, one Quranic principle that evades members of the Nation is the concept of brotherhood for all men. While this principle would be considered a foundational understanding of a traditional Islamic faith context, the impact of the social struggles in America has deemed it difficult to see white men in any other light than the devils they act like.

FAMILY SYSTEMS AS A CONSIDERING FACTOR

In examining family systems, one must seek to conceptualize emotional processes so that we can recognize them and, ultimately, let them serve rather than corrupt the purpose of our bonding together. Peter L. Steinke suggests that the goal of examining family systems, or system theory, centers on the awareness of the emotional state and not merely on understanding it. Steinke writes, "Understanding alone will not change these processes. But if understanding is translated into new ways of being and doing, emotional processes can be directed toward health and well-being as we live the divine vocation entrusted to us."[6]

In assessing Steinke's perspective, Steinke suggests that system theory is a valuable tool that aids FLG members through the stages of transformation. I understand system theory as "the study of society as a complex arrangement of elements, including individuals and their beliefs, as they relate to a whole."[7] Furthermore, Steinke writes, "System Theory is a way of conceptualizing reality. It organizes our thinking from a specific vantage point. System theory considers the interrelatedness of the parts. Instead of seeing isolated, unrelated parts, we look at the whole."[8] It is not enough to merely interpret the position/disposition of FLG members; we, the leadership of the local Black Baptist church, must process their intent.

To understand the family legacy group's social origins, the congregational leader must wear multiple hats—pastor, teacher, and social analyst. They should look beyond the typical perspective of satanic involvement and explore the psychosocial dynamics that impact Black individuals in their community. This research is essential because these very individuals are congregants in the church. To better understand the construction of social origins in this congregational context, I recommend referring to the social scientific models of the Black church outlined by Eric C. Lincoln and Lawrence H. Mamiya in their book *Down by the Riverside: Readings in African American Religion*, specifically the "Dialectical Model of the Black Church."

Lincoln and Mamiya draw upon the research of Hart M. Nelsen and Anne Kusener Nelson in "Black Church in the Sixties"

---

6. Steinke, *How Your Church Family Works*, loc. 133.
7. Encyclopedia Britannica, "Systems Theory."
8. Steinke, *How Your Church Family Works*, 33.

to bring attention to a specific Black Church model (the Compensatory Model) that aligns with my perspective on the congregational and community challenges faced by Wayside Baptist Church. This principle recognizes the psychosocial factors that shape the attitudes and actions of family legacy members within the church. Lincoln and Mamiya assert that

> the Black Church's main attraction is to give large masses of people, the opportunity for power, control, applause, and the claim within the group, which they do not receive in the larger society, as St. Clair, Drake, and Horace Cayton asserted in Black Metropolis. This view was also related to Gunnar Myrdal's perspective in An American Dilemma, that the black community is essentially pathological, and black culture is a distorted development of general American culture, so people compensate for this lack of a claim and lack of access to mainstream society in their institutions.[9]

While I understand Lincoln and Mamiya's position, the main attraction of the Black church/Black Baptist church should be Jesus. With all the things that African Americans experienced, encountered, and endured, the attractiveness of the Black Baptist church should be a savior who journeys with the pilgrim, who stands with the other, the left out, and brings liberation to the captive. The Black Baptist church should highlight the resilience of a Black woman who refused to leave Jesus without ensuring that her child would be healed. The Black Baptist church should highlight Simon of Cyrene, who was summoned to carry the cross of Jesus when he had no more strength to carry the cross the rest of the way. The Black Baptist church should highlight the Ethiopian eunuch who held a position of power, mastered several languages to conduct business along the trade routes from Ethiopia to Jerusalem, came to Jerusalem for worship, encountered Phillip on his way home, and was taught about Jesus and baptized. Consequently, while my suggestions are stirring for me, my view of attraction do not project power, popularity, or prestige in the church or the community.

9. Lincoln, "Dialectical Model," 329.

Social Origins of Family Legacy Group Members

In a social stratosphere where subjugation, demoralization, and injustice on a myriad of levels are a social constant for the Black body, opportunities for power and control are attractive. If this is the ploy that the Black Baptist church employs to make the Black Baptist church attractive, then in theory and practice, are we any different from the Nation of Islam, which posits a religious face with a Black nationalist functionality? Again, my assessment does not seek to project a negative image of the Nation. I am referencing an understanding of what we deem as markers of attraction to a religious group that does not poster the religion part of the religion on the marquee.

Although members of family legacy groups in Black Baptist congregations are a select group, the comparison of deconstructed social identities to congregational positions of prominence is accurate and valuable. It's important to note that this medium is not limited to Black men but offers an inclusive position to Black women. Pinn writes, "Gender construction took on an ephemeral quality compared to the heavy lifting accomplished by Black sensory difference. In short, Black women were first Black and then something resembling women (when the latter served the interests of Whites)."[10] Therefore, for some, the Black Baptist church is the only space where the Black body can experience a sense of social prestige. Although my focus is not on womanist social thought, it's crucial to acknowledge that Black women in the Black Baptist church face discrimination from two sides. They must confront the ever-present tensions associated with the social construct based on ethnicity as well as trauma and bias based on their gender identification in the Black Baptist church, despite possessing more education, experience, and skills than their male counterparts.

This approach lays the groundwork for the strategy I seek to establish as a starting point for the transformation process. Additionally, it provides knowledge concerning the intent of the decisions made by FLG members. It offers answers to the "why" questions we have concerning their thought processes and behaviors. When used correctly, system theory can work to remove

---

10. Pinn, *Understanding and Transforming*, 7.

the emotional reactions that typically exist as a response to oppositional behaviors and foster a position that the leadership of the local Black Baptist church can take, which sees the root of the problem instead of the individual exhibiting the oppositional behavior. While this approach takes on a more clinical approach to conflict resolution, it may be beneficial when attempting to develop an awareness of the conflicts in the local Black Baptist church. This concept often implies collaborating with or hiring other organizations that focus on analyzing and interpreting behaviors from a clinical or psychological perspective, rather than solely a spiritual one.

COMPARING OUR PAST EXPERIENCES TO OUR PRESENT BEHAVIORS

Dr. Joy DeGruy Leary, in *Post Traumatic Slave Syndrome*, asks, "What effect has our history had on our culture and our soul?"[11] History leaves a mark on both our emotions and psyche, shaping our thoughts and actions. Therefore, by exploring the social and congregational backgrounds of FLG members, one can delve into their history to identify social and congregational trends. Although new generations arise from this group over time, their fundamental social and congregational tendencies remain steadfast.

Reflecting on the experiences that have shaped us as Black individuals, what historical events influence our perception of ourselves and each other? Is there a correlation between the contrasting human and social actions of members within the Black Baptist church's family legacy group and the societal construct of racism in America? Could the social challenges outside of the Black church be an underlying force that fuels the social and congregational difficulties within the local Black Baptist church? Broadly speaking, I believe so. If the societal issues that plague us inform our identity and thought processes, then race, from a social standpoint, certainly impacts the Black Baptist church and

---

11. Leary, *Post Traumatic Slave Syndrome*, 111.

the community where the church exists. According to Anthony B. Pinn, "as race is a social construct, how those 'raced' bodies are marked and distinguished is also a matter of social construction."[12]

The social construct in America has emotional and psychological consequences that affect African Americans and their social conditions. Although some individuals attend the Black Baptist church, societal factors influence their perception of society and God. Many seek to view God beyond the confines of Scripture, hoping that the liberating God of the Bible can be present in their current context. This way, individuals can also experience liberation from today's social injustices. Black bodies in America are historically disenfranchised, and the markers of identification, while misinterpreted, have been constructed to perpetuate trauma in Black bodies pre- and post-conversation. Although seldom discussed in some Black Baptist churches, these effects are vital to understanding individuals in the congregation who comprise FLG members and individuals who collectively include the assembly.

Referencing Malcolm, his lived experiences and encounters depict how social conditioning impacts identity formation and socialization. Malcolm's foundation was Garveyism/Black Nationalist thought, which created a healthy self-empowering identity formation contrary to how whiteness attempted to frame Black identity at that time. Therefore, his connection to the Nation of Islam during his early adulthood appeared natural, reflecting the foundation of his personal experiences. The Nation of Islam exercised a social/religious interference to combat the American social construct that sought to exploit Black bodies through economic deprivation, dehumanization, social injustice, and racial oppression. The leaders of the Nation believed that self-determination was the key to survival. Thus, they sought to establish a power system and structure to free the Black race from white interference and control.

As the oldest grassroots Black Muslim movement in America, the Nation of Islam created a theology and praxis of liberation that was fashioned in response to the Western interpretation of

---

12. Pinn, Pinn, *Understanding and Transforming*, 6.

Christianity intermingled with white supremacist ideology. While I do not wish to debate the tenets of white supremacist thought with Christianity in this book, I do want to address the position of the American social construct, how it impacted Black bodies in America, and the position taken by the Nation of Islam that presented this organization in a light depicted as oppositional to one group of people and supportive to another. Thus, the social conditions of America, which have not changed much since the Nation's formation, prompted this religious/social group to remain in a constant state of survival.

Although Malcolm had a family dynamic that provided a positive reaffirmation concerning his Black identity, in the church, positive reaffirmation often came from congregational leaders, church mothers and missionaries, and female members in the church. While most pastors are embraced by the congregation, overtime, some tensions occur if the agenda of the congregational leader and FLG members differ. In these instances, FLG members may assess the views of new congregational leaders as antagonistic to a family legacy group narrative that seeks to maintain their modality. Efforts to introduce new viewpoints aimed at transforming the church are seen as attempts to undermine members of the family legacy group in the sole arena that offers social influence, privilege, and status.

The Black Baptist church leaders seeking to understand the reasoning behind FLG members' actions and beliefs can find answers in their social backgrounds. It is important to note that the tensions within the congregation related to FLG members are not always a result of deliberate contradictions but rather stem from social trauma, racism, and fears of losing their unique identity. Examining social origins allows for a broader perspective on developing conflict resolution in the congregation, shedding light on behavioral origins of Black individuals in the Black Baptist church. Our goal is to guide the leadership and FLG members toward a solution that fosters community and inclusivity.

While transformation is attainable, in a setting where trauma is a core element, the notion of trust becomes difficult to navigate.

An effective strategist must engage with this social or congregational environment by recognizing the various complexities, such as race, different forms of inequality, and identity issues, that all play a role in the potential resistance encountered during the process. To contribute to someone's transformation effectively, we must "listen carefully and sensitively to what the situation is saying—what the thoughts, desires, and actions of the people seem to convey before deciding on a plan of action."[13]

---

13. Smith, "Relational Self," 35.

CHAPTER 3

Teaching as a Tool for Transformation

THE EFFECTS OF PERCEPTION and trauma present difficulties in congregations and social environments, yet these do not need to follow a single, reactive pattern. We should promote a new reality that draws on survival strategies and integrates a framework for congregations and communities. Herein lies the tension—the implications of critical consciousness run counter to the social dynamics of acceptance in congregational and social life. To put it simply, members of the Black Baptist church often find it challenging to openly express their thoughts or hold an opinion that may differ from the power dynamic in the church.

The typical role of individuals in the congregational and social space is diverse, influenced by their role and, for some, by their ability to express themselves. However, as individuals are not confined to the natural, biological sphere but also participate in the creative dimension, they can intervene and bring about change if they dare to do so. This pursuit of rediscovery and action stems from transformative teaching. Transformative teaching works to reshape current biblical and organizational understandings into a new comprehension of governance and practices within congregational and social contexts. We begin by evaluating an operational definition of transformative teaching to lay the groundwork for my theory.

Teaching as a Tool for Transformation

What is transformative teaching? I will define my concept of transformative teaching by briefly assessing Jack Mezirow's transformative learning theory as my primary source for understanding transformative teaching. Mezirow grounds his transformative learning theory in critical reflection and self-reflection on assumptions, along with critical discourse. Mezirow's theory, a beacon of enlightenment, manifests itself in three dynamics: instrumental—how learners best acquire information; dialogic—when and where this learning can best occur; and self-reflective—why the learner is engaging with the information, providing a clear and comprehensive understanding of the transformative learning process.

From this perspective, transformative learning involves gaining new knowledge and reassessing our previous thoughts and comprehension. It entails a substantial and deep alteration in our worldview as we acquire more information and insights. This type of learning does not discard our earlier perceptions but instead leads to a fundamental shift in our understanding of the world. Consequently, our social references are altered, creating a new paradigm that is based on potential rather than trauma. To engage in this methodology in ways that will be mutually beneficial to the teacher and student, one must reference Mezirow's transformative learning theory but implement the teaching techniques of bell hooks and Paulo Freire. Mezirow, while useful, offers limitations in execution based on his methodology's close association with what Freire describes as the banking system. Thus, I turn to the teaching strategies of bell hooks and Paulo Freire as outlined in hooks's *Teaching to Transgress* and Freire's *Pedagogy of the Oppressed*. Despite its traditional academic application, I am convinced that these methodologies are beneficial for teaching in congregational settings.

A DIFFERENT WAY

Let us begin by exploring a mutuality learning concept that may be beneficial in transformative environments. Although the teacher may be responsible for developing curriculum and direction for the learning space, education's purpose should be to provide liberation for everyone involved. Through this approach, teachers and students become channels for one another, drawing on knowledge, research, and experience in ways that liberate and empower all participants in their educational endeavors. Thus, liberation-based learning is not a one-sided experience where information is shared by the teacher and later regurgitated by the student. Instead, its contribution to freeing students and educators creates an environment conducive to shared critical thinking, empowerment, and societal transformation.

For this type of engagement and outcome to occur, teaching must be a "practice of freedom."[1] The purpose of a learning environment should be to empower individuals rather than merely disseminating information. For the congregational space, teachers must come to the learning environment conscious that those who engage in this space are looking for answers that will help them navigate through the challenges life presents. Hooks says, "To teach in a manner that respects and cares for the souls of our students is essential if we are to provide the necessary conditions where learning can most deeply and intimately begin."[2] Hooks emphasizes the need for teachers to prioritize students' emotional and well-being needs. This premise should serve as a foundation for instructors in all learning spheres. Furthermore, hooks highlights the significance of cultivating an environment that supports inner growth, which is essential for promoting profound and meaningful learning experiences. If this ideology is a tenet for academic learning spaces, how much more should it be a methodological tenet for instructors in congregational environments?

In several congregational learning spaces, learning is not depicted in ways that employ a holistic model of learning. Often, the congregational learning space associates itself with what Freire calls the banking system. In his book *Pedagogy of the Oppressed*, Freire offers content regarding the banking system. For Freire, the banking system model functions in ways that assess the student

---

1. hooks, *Teaching to Transgress*, 13.
2. hooks, *Teaching to Transgress*, 13.

Teaching as a Tool for Transformation

as a container who receives information from the all-knowing teacher. This educational model's objective is intake and regurgitation, not critical thinking. Freire asserts that "the outstanding characteristic of this narrative education, then, is the sonority of words, not their transforming power."[3]

Freire's concept of the banking system in education portrays students as vessels into which an all-knowing teacher deposits information. This educational approach prioritizes memorization and repetition over critical analysis. According to Freire, the banking model of education reflects societal dynamics, serving the interests of the oppressors within that society. In a manner akin to being handed pieces of fish without ever learning to catch fish themselves, students absorb information. If this is the primary learning system in place in most of our Black churches, then I assert that several Black churches utilize the banking system as their primary style of teaching. How then do we transform our Black Baptist churches into a transformative environment? According to Freire, "dialogue" is the answer.[4] In order for a dialogue to take place, congregational teachers need to give others the chance to voice their thoughts. This chance for verbal expression is found within the framework of the ongoing discussion. Freire posits "if it is in speaking their word that people, by naming the world, transform it, dialogue imposes itself as the way by which they achieve significance as human beings. Dialogue is thus an existential necessity."[5]

Herein lies a contrasting position. In several Black Baptist churches, as stated earlier in this section, critical thinking is not a customary practice. Thus, verbal exchange/engagement is seldom practiced in the Black Baptist church. If/when there are voices who seek to engage in the lesson—altering the educational landscape from monologue to dialogue—in certain spaces, there is resistance because dialogue does not associate itself with the status quo for congregational learning. Because of this notion,

---

3. Freire, *Pedagogy of the Oppressed*, loc. 976.
4. Freire, *Pedagogy of the Oppressed*, loc. 1251.
5. Freire, *Pedagogy of the Oppressed*, loc. 1251.

several individuals merely sit and take in what is presented, never attempting to engage or offer an alternative example, whether its source is research-based or experience-based. Freire asserts that "dialogue cannot exist, however, in the absence of a profound love for the world and for people."[6] This brings us back to hooks's assertion of care. Whether we use the term care or love, care/love must rest at the core of what we do. Assessing the actions of God in John 3:16, it was "love" that served as the "why" of sending his son to redeem humankind.[7] As teachers, we need to be intentional about what we share, the spaces we create, and the opportunity for mutual exchange. This act of social empowerment through congregational and social intervention directly results from transformative teaching.

HURDLES TO LEARNING IN BLACK BAPTIST CHURCHES

Although I am convinced that education serves as an effective means of transformation within Black Baptist churches, a significant issue faced by many of these congregations is the lack of engagement in reading the Bible or related materials outside of the congregational arena. This disengagement extends to participation in the educational aspects of church life, which plays a role in reshaping the congregation. Researchers from Pew Research Center suggest that "40% of Black adults engage in reading scripture outside of religious services multiple times a week or more frequently, while 15% do so about once a week or a few times a month, and 46% rarely or never participate in this activity."[8] If biblical learning aids the transformation process, yet congregational learning spaces are the least attended by congregants, what needs to happen to shift the pendulum? What does the church need to do to encourage members to engage or reengage in the learning spaces

6. Freire, *Pedagogy of the Oppressed*, loc. 1265.
7. John 3:16.
8. Mohamed, "Religious Practices," 4.

of congregational life? Is the study of the biblical text interesting enough to hold our attention, or are those who teach in the Black church not versed enough to make congregational learning intriguing?

After conversing with a few Black pastors of several denominational arenas, it became evident that most concurred on a primary reason for the low attendance at weekly Bible studies and Sunday school classes within the Black church community. They perceive these gatherings (Bible study and Sunday school) as more enriching than entertaining, which leads to a lack of participation from many members. While there are a few Black Baptist churches that offer a praise and worship segment before Bible study, this addition to the learning space is not a typical practice in the Black Baptist church space. Often, the addition of praise of worship prior to study transitions the learning moment over time to more of a midweek service.

After speaking with a few members of several Black Baptist churches, their assessment appears contrasting to the perception of the pastors. From the vantage point of the young adults to middle-aged adults, Bible study and Sunday school struggle with attendance because the teaching methodology is not intriguing. While the message of the Bible is universal, some members have suggested that the teaching style is often dry, stale, and offers no association to current theological issues and social challenges. For the senior saints, their lack of attending Bible study has more to do with coming outside at night than it does with the lesson plans of the teachers. Additionally, several of the senior saints suggested that they get their lesson during the preaching moment on Sunday, so there is no need to come out during the week to attend Bible study.

Within a typical Black Baptist church environment, there are no prerequisites for teachers to acquire formal education as a preparatory practice. Thus, we end up reading through a booklet or lesson plan that is general enough in its formation but seldom unpacked in ways that offer specificity to our social and cultural experiences. If we do not have teachers in the Black Baptist church who do the work to make the lessons useful to our social/cultural experiences and theological needs, how will Bible study, Sunday school, and small group learning spaces foster the spark needed to pique our curiosity? As a result, since formal education is not required for our congregational teachers, some views on biblical interpretation within the Black Baptist church are akin to the personal piety or social standing of the instructors. Therefore, the more devout you seem, or depending on the church family you relate to, the more people are persuaded of the teacher's grasp of Scripture.

TRANSITION

When instructors are well-prepared and dedicated to empowering and nurturing their students, the potential for change and growth becomes attainable. Although transitions can occur in environments like Wayside, they may encounter both internal and external obstacles. Let us look at an encounter at the Wayside Baptist Church and the future reformed members of the family legacy group. As Rev. White introduced new teachings to the church, a few of the younger members of the family legacy group took a keen interest. Although they have not displayed their interest openly, they have been reflecting on and applying what they have learned. Over time, they have witnessed the positive impact of implementing these teachings. While they are still considered the next generation of leaders within the family legacy group, they are now grappling with the group's inclination to uphold the status quo in contrast to what they have learned from Rev. White.

The internal struggle was two-fold for the future reformed FLG members. On the one hand, these individuals had to grapple with publicly supporting positions that do not align with the power dynamics. Even if their intentions do not align with the new congregational leader's stance, they may face pushback for presenting perspectives that do not exclusively endorse existing views. Although some individuals no longer agree with the ruling party in these moments, they remain silent due to fear and the

Teaching as a Tool for Transformation

possibility of social ridicule or confrontation. Another position suggests that resistance occurs to opposing stances in cases where a congregation has a history of short-term tenured leadership. In cases like Wayside, it is seen as problematic to take an approach that contradicts the power dynamic, as the power dynamic typically outlasts transient leaders. While selected leaders do not intend to be transient when they arrive at a church, they rarely last more than three to four years in cases like this. Suppose a member of the family legacy group dares to take a different position. In that case, it often leads to social and congregational disassociation.

As an example, there was an incident that occurred at Wayside. The family legacy group knew they were in over their heads, but they refused to let Rev. White help them out of this crisis. Instead of siding with the members of the family legacy group and keeping the information to themselves, a few group members provided Rev. White with the necessary information needed to rectify the situation before it escalated. Although Rev. White's assistance saved the congregation resources in hindsight, the family legacy group perceived these individuals' actions as antithetical to what they believed was proper protocol and functioning for their created system. As a result, these individuals, now deemed untrustworthy by the family legacy group, were disassociated and ostracized from other FLG members. They eventually left Wayside and connected to a different, mutuality-friendly, nondenominational church.

Looking to the experiences of Malcolm X—in the past, Malcolm was resolute concerning the teachings and message of the Honorable Elijah Muhammad and the Nation's practices. Eventually, Malcolm began testing Muhammad's doctrines against his understanding of Islam. While Malcolm did not say that Muhammad's words were wrong, he left the proverbial door open to the idea that Elijah Muhammad's teachings were not above the scrutiny of human reason.[9] Malcolm began to transition internally. As an inquirer of orthodox doctrine, Malcolm wrestled with what was cultivating in him (orthodox Islam) and what he was associated with (the Nation of Islam). According to DeCaro, "the real issue,

---

9. DeCaro, *On the Side*, loc. 160.

then, was how long Malcolm could continue parroting Muhammad's doctrines and live with his own growing need to express his religious, social, and political independence."[10]

DEVELOPING A NEW NORMAL

In evaluating the effects of teaching and exposure to new information, looking at the experiences of those who would eventually become reformed FLG members, can new information inform and transform a person or group without causing disassociation? I believe the answer to this question is context-specific. Please assess the following as a potential outcome of two individuals from the family legacy group, now reformed: Consider two individuals positively impacted by new information. Furthermore, envision these two individuals possessing contrasting personality traits. The first individual is assertive and up-front about their beliefs. Often, the more outspoken of the two is heard but still socially rejected. Either the results of this individual produce a continuation of social/congregational contention, or they end up leaving the church due to unreconcilable differences. The second individual is also positively affected but tends to be more passive. Despite disagreeing with the existing power dynamics, they feel trapped within the system, holding onto hope that those in power will eventually do the right thing. They often find themselves trapped in a congregational paradox, waiting in vain but trying to persuade others to endure the same self-centered behavior they endure, which usually never alters.

Let us look at a transitional period in Malcolm X's life between pre-hajj and hajj as an example of developing a new normal comparable to what sometimes happens and what can happen in the Black church. For Malcolm, an association with a new understanding of belief and practice that would revolutionize his faith and lived experiences occurred before his pilgrimage to the Holy

---

10. DeCaro, *On the Side*, loc. 201.

Land. Long before Malcolm could come to Mecca, Mecca seemed to have come to Malcolm.[11]

Malcolm was no longer a pupil of the Honorable Elijah Muhammad. Malcolm eventually became an inquirer of what some traditional Islamic Muslims would consider true Islam. Malcolm's initiation into traditional Islamic thought came from a Sudanese Muslim student named Ahmed Osman. For Ahmed, true Islam made no distinction of color—all men who subscribed to the oneness of God could become a brother. Ahmed challenged Malcolm, not in a way to embarrass him, but in ways that informed him of what was right and true. After their initial encounter, Malcolm and Ahmed remained close acquaintances. After frequent Islamic literature exchanges, Malcolm requested Ahmed's explanation of Quranic exegesis. As their friendship grew, Ahmed encouraged Malcolm to make hajj. Ahmed knew the experience of hajj would be beneficial for Malcolm during this period of transition.

Malcolm dove deeper into orthodox teachings. Up until now, Malcolm lived as a Black nationalist. Soon, Malcolm would become an orthodox Muslim. Being expelled from the Nation of Islam allowed Malcolm to shift from an ideology rooted in racial trauma and internal religious conflicts, characterized by animosity and opposition toward white people, to one of openness, seeing traditional Islam as a faith accessible to individuals outside of his ethnicity.

Malcolm's lived experiences and encounters reflect a premise offered by the apostle Paul in his letter to the Roman church. This canonical thought suggests that the events of life are synergetic. Thus, the events that led to his disassociation from the Nation of Islam "worked together"[12] to open a new road for Malcolm, inevitably introducing him to an uncharted critical discourse: Sunni Islam. Evaluating the lived experiences and encounters of Malcolm X and future reformed legacy group members, the larger group (the NOI and the ruling members of the family legacy group) remained resolute in their position. While one can suggest that the

---

11. DeCaro, *On the Side*, loc. 203.
12. Rom 8:28.

position of Muhammad and the Nation, along with the position of the family legacy group, may have merit—in a broader sense, both groups maintained a survival modality birthed out of pain, trauma, and social/congregational power.

AN ENVIRONMENT CONDUCIVE FOR LEARNING

Pedagogy is critical to the transformation process of individuals undergoing reshaping. Pedagogy is the method and practice of teaching, especially an academic subject or theoretical concept. Focused instructors must approach the learning context with the belief that advocates to the learner that an aspect of their role is sacred. Their pedagogy must offer a belief that suggests that their interest in engaging is not fixated on sharing information only but constructed in a way that moves the instructor to participate in the holistic growth of the learner.[13] Thus, a care component for the learner must accompany the facilitator's knowledge. This premise is vital to the learning process.

Assessing this approach, let us first look at Malcolm X and Dr. Shawarbi's interactions as examples. In Marable's book *Malcolm X: A Life of Reinvention*, he offers context to the interactions between Malcolm X and Dr. Shawarbi. Although their initial engagement was in October 1960 at an NOI-sponsored event, Malcolm and Dr. Shawarbi kept in sporadic touch until his silencing was over.[14] Additionally, Marable says,

> Shawarbi was crucial to Malcolm's development in other ways. Persistently, but without confrontation, he challenged Malcolm to rethink his race-based worldview, admitting that many orthodox Muslims also fell short of the color-blind ideals they professed. He finally convinced Malcolm that the Qur'an, as conceived in the recitations of the Prophet Muhammad, was racially egalitarian—which meant that whites, through their

---

13. hooks, *Teaching to Transgress*, 13–22.
14. Marable, *Malcolm X*, loc. 222.

submission to Allah, would become spiritual brothers and sisters to Blacks.[15]

One can imply that Dr. Shawarbi's pedagogy provided Malcolm with patience, non-judgment, openness, and understanding. Malcolm was interested in discovering the truth, and Dr. Shawarbi grounded his exposure. Although a few groups deemed Malcolm's views controversial, bold, and confrontational before his interactions with Dr. Shawarbi, none of these perspectives about Malcolm deterred Dr. Shawarbi from their mutual engagement of traditional Quranic understanding. Malcolm immersed himself in traditional Islamic teaching. He was so engrossed that he sometimes even cried while passages of the Holy Quran were read.[16] If bell hooks were to evaluate Dr. Shawarbi as an instructor, she would consider him a teacher who dared to transgress boundaries.

My experiences of critical pedagogy in the congregational context do not mirror the experiences of Malcolm. Although dialogue occurs during teaching moments, seldom are those moments used for self-reflection on matters that call for critical thinking and evaluation. While there is always room for this premise to change in the Black church, critical thinking as a practice has its limits in a few churches like Wayside. To this end, the principles of critical pedagogy can shift congregational paradigms. To educate as the practice of freedom is a way of teaching that anyone can learn.[17]

JESUS AS TEACHER

Let us use the example of the historical Jesus to support this claim of teaching as a tool for transformation. My reference to Jesus will not investigate the varying complexities of his description in canonical writings or theological comments made by scholars of varying perspectives. I aim to use the historical Jesus in a way that will centralize itself on a singular designation: teacher. My

---

15. Marable, *Malcolm X*, loc. 223.
16. DeCaro, *On the Side*, loc. 202–3.
17. hooks, *Teaching to Transgress*, 13.

reference to the historical Jesus offers a depiction of the Jesus in New Testament Scripture who lived as a human in a human context. While each Gospel writer wrote to a specific audience with a particular message, central to their writings was an understanding of Jesus as a teacher. Jesus held no affiliations with the Pharisees or the Sadducees, the two main Jewish religious sects presented to us in the New Testament Scripture. Jesus was a carpenter by trade whose focus morphed from constructing tables to reconstructing lives.

Many examples throughout Scripture speak to the impact of Jesus' pedagogy. Jesus was known for setting the stage that fostered transformation in some shape or form for those who engaged with his teachings. While his teaching style was unconventional, it reached people where they were. Let us reference a few examples of his encounters and the responses to these encounters. On one occasion, Jesus witnesses a crowd nearby. He and his disciples rested on a mountain as he began to teach. For two chapters, Jesus unpacks truths and expounds the law in ways his listeners had never heard before. Nearing the conclusion of his Sermon on the Mount, those who listened to his teachings said "he taught as one who had authority, and not as their teachers of the law."[18]

On another occasion, Jesus meets up with a Pharisee named Nicodemus at night. During their dialogue, Jesus shares the principles of the kingdom with Nicodemus. Confused by the concept, Nicodemus asked, "How can someone be born again when they are old? Surely, they cannot enter a second time into their mother's womb."[19] Jesus questions Nicodemus's ignorance concerning being "born again" as a concept, seeing that he is "Israel's teacher."[20] In my last description, Jesus speaks to the Pharisees, tax collectors, and sinners. In this three-part monologue in Luke 15, Jesus shares the heart of a loving God for the lost in ways that stand against Pharisaic judgments concerning Jesus' choice to associate himself with tax collectors and sinners. Thus, through mountaintop

---

18. Matt 7:29.
19. John 3:4.
20. John 3:10.

sermons, nighttime one-on-one conversations, or even parables, Jesus' pedagogy during his time was highly impactful and life-altering. As members of a non-Jewish congregation, some associate Blacks as gentiles by way of origin.

Thus, for some, our association with Christianity affiliates itself with Jesus the Christ as Savior and God, not the historical Jesus, a Jewish follower of the Torah's training in moral laws. Even though we are recipients of the filling of the Spirit of God, similar to the Corinthian church, some Black churches encounter challenges with issues centered around immaturity, division, and immorality. While we aim to transform lives in the Black church, Christ as the divine entity is problematic as a working example of how humanity lives out Christianity. The concept of Christ speaks to his divinity. Even in our best attempts, becoming divine in a human context is unattainable by humanity's measures. Jesus was not Christian. He was Jewish. However, we defer to the teachings of Paul, which are empire-specific to the teachings of Jesus, which spoke against the empire.

I am not suggesting that the Black Baptist church converts to Judaism. I am asking the following question: in what ways does the historical Jesus serve as an example of Christian living apart from his association with an ethic-heavy Jewish religious context and practice? We must understand that Judaism is a behavior-heavy religious sect. Simply put, the tenets of Judaism emphasize the practice of the law to this day. Thus, it focuses not on one's beliefs but on how an individual behaves.

If Jesus is the example for the Christian, understanding his Jewishness is vital to a richer, fuller understanding of Christianity. The pushback to this notion associates itself with the Jerusalem Council dispute. When conversations between Paul and Peter, from Peter's perspective, suggested that an association with Jesus held no validity apart from the practices of Jesus, tension arose for the gentile believer. Thus, the suggestion of circumcision emphasized behavior, not just beliefs. Circumcision was a covenantal act dating back to the days of Abram. It was a sign of a lasting bond between God, Abram, and his offspring. Although Peter and Paul created a working agreement for the gentile Christians, several of Paul's messages to gentile believers address challenges associated with behavior, not belief. We must remember that historically, Jesus did not do away with the law; he fulfilled it. However, Jesus' behavioral practices as a Jew did not serve as a standard of living for his gentile followers.

In the Black Baptist church, some challenges relate to behavior, not belief exclusively. While education to the congregational leader is encouraged within the Black Baptist church, the focus is theology, not ethics. We push the context of Christianity as a believing dynamic, but we seldom associate an ethic that matches the tenets of our belief system. Why is the concept of ethics in the church both a valued and unpracticed practice in the Black Baptist church? For the Black Baptist church, the answer is simple. Ethics is valued because its fundamental stance, particularly in Black Baptist churches, is exclusive to the leader instead of inclusive to all Christians in the congregational context. When moments of tension occur between the leader and the congregation, the premise of frustration is often assessed as a matter of behavior, not belief.

The responsibility of Christian ethical expression is usually central to the congregational leader, not the congregant. Thus, what should be an inclusive practice for all is relegated to an exclusive practice for some. If we teach that the pastor is the only one responsible for being ethical, we present a doctrine unfounded on Scripture, polity, and congregational governance. Additionally, this premise offers a false, partial, and misleading interpretation of Christianity. Stances like this foster division in the church because it implies that the pastor is the only entity that must live up to an ethical standard. While I am not suggesting that the congregational leader does not have to live up to a standard, I am suggesting that the standard of ethics should be a byproduct of our rights as Christians, not exclusive to the role of the pastor in the congregational context.

Furthermore, seeing that the formation of several Black Baptist churches results from congregational disagreement and disconnection, the Black Baptist church has grappled with identity

TEACHING AS A TOOL FOR TRANSFORMATION

matters since its inception. Because Black individuals themselves have frequently been unsure of their identity, and because the Black church is itself a creature of the countercurrents of American racial proclivities, the Black church has not always been without ambivalence in its understanding of what it is and why.[21] If we subscribe to this premise as truth, it supports the need for teaching in the Black Baptist church.

Where do we start when assessing teaching as a tool for transformation? Do we begin by reshaping survival modalities exclusively, or do we start by addressing the issues that lay at the foundation of our belief system? What will transformative teaching unearth, and how will that change the lives of future reformed FLG members and alter the identity of the entire church altogether? Several Black Baptist churches are autonomous and, as such, are self-governing and self-directing. If the Black Baptist church is unclear concerning who she is, how effective will she be as a self-governing entity? Furthermore, suppose those who make up the ruling body in the church ground their understanding of governance on survival modalities. What image will the church depict to its congregants and the community where she exists? Can the church reimagine her identity in ways that exist outside the purview of trauma? Are the people open to a form of teaching that challenges them to see themselves in a new way?

I believe that a well-prepared instructor, who grounds their teaching approach with the spirit of care, can cultivate a learning environment that can foster transformation. While there are a myriad of topics and methodologies that can be useful, for the Black Baptist church, I believe that Lent as a taught practice in the church during the Lenten season and pilgrimage as a reimagined concept for the Black Baptist church can contribute to the transformation process. While I do not assert that transformation will be immediate, I do believe that transformation is inevitable. I will cover these entities (Lenten practices and a reimagination of pilgrimage) in the upcoming chapter.

---

21. Lincoln, "Power in the Black Church," 3–21.

CHAPTER 4

Right Beliefs and Behaviors for the Congregation and Her Leader

CAN THE ACTIVE EMBODIMENT of our faith positively lead to profound personal transformation? Indeed, actively embodying faith can significantly alter a person on ethical, spiritual, emotional, and even social levels. When faith transcends mere intellectual belief and is deliberately practiced in everyday life through acts of compassion, justice, service, forgiveness, prayer, or meditation, it becomes a powerful shaping force. In *Mediations of the Heart*, Thurman suggests that "the ability to know what is the right thing to do in a given circumstance is a sheer gift of God. The element of gift is inherent in the process of decision."[1] This concept highlights Thurman's focus on the internal journey as the foundation for external actions and ethical involvement. Moreover, it suggests that our choices are made with purpose when our actions aim to bring about change in ourselves and those we encounter.

Living according to one's faith necessitates aligning actions with fundamental values. This deliberate practice often results in enhanced moral clarity and consistency as individuals become more aware of their decisions and their effects on others. As stated in Jas 2:17, "Faith, if it has no works, is dead."[2] This biblical concept

---

1. Thurman, *Meditations of the Heart*, 79.
2. Jas 2:17.

implies that faith only truly comes alive and initiates change when it is put into action—first internally, then externally. Embodied faith frequently involves spiritual disciplines like prayer, fasting, worship, and service, which gradually mold one's inner character, foster resilience, and deepen one's connection with the divine.

Particularly in liberation theology and Black religious thought, embodied faith extends beyond the personal to the communal and political, prompting individuals to stand with the oppressed and advocate for justice. Embodied faith serves as a living testament that can inspire others and nurture transformative communities. It shifts the focus from doctrine to relational presence and lived integrity.

In this chapter, I aim to explore a topic that is rarely addressed in the Black Baptist church: religious ethics. How does engaging in religious ethics facilitate the transformation of FLG members and churchgoers? What actions should leaders and change agents within the Black Baptist church take to assist in this transformation? The ethics of care provides a lens for scrutinizing social policies, practices, and relationships in our daily lives, offering a chance to rejuvenate or metamorphose them. To facilitate such transformations, it's crucial to identify and confront the barriers that obstruct this process. For transformation to take root, it's imperative that leaders and change agents not only understand but also actively embrace an ethic that fosters transformation. My stance doesn't advocate for congregational leaders and change agents to subject themselves to the hardships of congregants and community members grappling with trauma. Instead, they should assess the situation and ensure their conduct does not impede the transformation process.

With this premise at the heart of this chapter, I want to reference a few social encounters between Sunni Muslims and Malcolm X in Jeddah. We can draw insights from Malcolm's interactions with Sunni Muslims in the Middle East, which showcase how one's ethics can contribute to a reshaping process for an individual engaged in social and religious reform. Despite their differing religious beliefs and practices, Sunni Muslims in the context that I seek to reference offer a valuable model for Black Baptist church leaders who seek to inspire positive behavior and values within their community and congregation. In essence, we observe the enactment of religious teachings and values in a manner that challenges and reshapes societal stereotypes and frameworks.

I do not intend to present Islamic theological perspectives as a benchmark for Christian leaders. While interfaith engagement has validity, my objective in this segment is to evaluate the conduct/ethics of white Sunni Muslims from Malcolm X's lived experiences in Mecca and how their religious values, despite their white ethnicity, offered Malcolm a unique social experience that played a role in Malcolm's transformation. Similarly, I aim to motivate Black Baptist church leaders to incorporate religious ethics into daily routines for personal reflection and pastoral duties, which can support the transformation of church and community members seeking spiritual and congregational renewal. To set the stage for my analysis, I would like to start by establishing a foundational understanding of the term "religious ethics." As I intend to reference the experiences of Malcolm X, I am considering religious ethics as a comprehensive interpretation of ethics useful for Christianity and Islam as religious traditions.

RELIGIOUS ETHICS EXPLAINED

Religious ethics can be understood as the moral principles and values derived from religious traditions, beliefs, and teachings that guide individuals and communities in making ethical decisions and shaping their behavior. It involves interpreting sacred texts, doctrines, and spiritual practices to address moral dilemmas and foster societal well-being while aligning with the foundational tenets of the faith. Religious ethics often emphasize the relationship between humanity and the divine, as well as interpersonal conduct rooted in compassion, justice, and integrity. Ronald M. Green, in "Religion and Moral Reason: A New Method for Comparative

Study," asserts, "Religious ethics is a systematic, comparative, and critical reflection on the moral dimensions of religious traditions."[3]

Religious ethics often stem from fundamental theological beliefs, such as the nature of the divine, human purpose, and the concepts of good and evil, and are influenced by historical, cultural, and philosophical contexts. They may be articulated in sacred authoritative traditions and embodied practices, e.g., rituals, charitable acts, and codes of conduct. While religious ethics may intersect with secular moral philosophies in areas like justice or compassion, they typically claim a transcendent foundation for moral principles and often involve spiritual or eschatological motivations, such as salvation, enlightenment, or divine judgment. These ethical systems can be examined comparatively, analyzing similarities and differences across traditions, or within a specific tradition, and are studied for both their internal consistency and their practical implications in fields like religion, law, politics, medicine, ecology, and human rights.

In a world that often operates without religious influence, the ethical principles derived from various faiths encounter numerous obstacles. Factors such as social diversity, political views, cultural relativism, universalism, modernization, and secularization all contribute to the difficulties faced by religious ethics. Religious scriptures and moral teachings are frequently subject to various interpretations, which can result in differing opinions within religious groups about what is deemed ethical. These religious ethical standards might clash with secular or other cultural moral systems, prompting debates about universal notions of right and wrong. As societies evolve, traditional religious moral codes may appear at odds with modern ethical dilemmas. Religious ethics often assert an absolute truth, potentially leading to conflict or violence in diverse societies where multiple ethical systems exist. David Hollenbach asserts,

> Religious ethics do not exist in a vacuum; they are embedded in social, cultural, and political contexts that shape their interpretation and application. The challenge

3. Green, *Religion and Moral Reason*, 5.

is that these contexts are often marked by inequality, exclusion, and power imbalances, which means that religious moral discourse can either reinforce or resist unjust social structures.[4]

To deepen our understanding of religious ethics, it is essential to examine the influence of power dynamics. These dynamics are crucial in determining which ethical interpretations are given precedence, who holds the authority to speak, and how justice is either pursued or obstructed. How can we then evaluate religious ethics from feminist, liberationist, and interfaith perspectives? Is it possible to develop an interpretation or framework that addresses the social challenges of race, gender, and class in a way that is acceptable to everyone?

Religious authorities frequently possess the ability to determine what is considered ethically permissible, which can potentially suppress opposing viewpoints or modern interpretations. Disparities in power may result in ethical manipulation, where those in authority mold doctrines for personal or organizational benefit. Historically, power dynamics within numerous religious traditions have marginalized women and LGBTQ+ individuals, impacting those whose ethical perspectives are either highlighted or silenced. Feminist theologians and ethicists contend that interpretations dominated by men often skew the inclusive ethical vision inherent in many faiths.

According to Margaret A. Farley,

> Religious ethical traditions have too often been shaped by male-dominated interpretations that marginalize women's experiences. Feminist ethics insists that any adequate moral theology must begin with the lived realities of women and challenge structures of domination.[5]

Missionary endeavors and colonial domination frequently imposed prevailing religious ethics on indigenous communities, ignoring local moral frameworks. Postcolonial ethics critiques the

---

4. Hollenbach, *Common Good*, 3.
5. Farley, *Just Love*, 213.

use of religion to justify exploitation and cultural erasure. Political regimes can exploit religious ethics to legitimize authority or suppress dissent. Ethical teachings might be selectively employed to rationalize war, nationalism, or social control. Wealthier religious entities or individuals may interpret ethics in ways that maintain their privileges while sidelining the poor or working class. Liberation theology opposes this by emphasizing ethics focused on the oppressed and advocating for justice. Gutiérrez posits, "The ethical imperative of faith is to stand with the oppressed. Ethics divorced from the lived struggle for justice becomes an instrument of the status quo rather than a means of liberation."[6]

LIVING IT OUT

In Louis A. DeCaro Jr.'s *On the Side of My People: The Religious Life of Malcolm X*, he writes,

> Malcolm noted that the white Muslims in the East were much different from American whites since Islam had removed the "white from their minds," and since these white Muslims were so free from color prejudice, Malcolm said, it allowed him to remove the "Negro" from his mind—with the result that all attitudes and behaviors had changed for the better.[7]

Looking at Malcolm, we see that he experienced an ethic lived out positively. The Sunni Muslims he engaged with lived out their faith. It was not a social act scripted for those making hajj. This was who they were. Malcolm first witnessed this premise through his encounters with Osman and Shawarbi in the States. Now, in Jeddah on his way to Mecca, he understood through social/religious engagement that whiteness is not universal. It is a construct. DeCaro suggests that "the essence of Sunni Islam is not found in mere doctrinal purity, nor literal orthodoxy, but in loyalty to the

---

6. Gutiérrez, *Theology of Liberation*, xxv.
7. DeCaro, *On the Side*, loc. 209.

Muslim community and its traditions."[8] One of the traditions of orthodox Islam is the notion of brotherhood for all humanity, regardless of race. Thus, when white Sunnis encountered Malcolm, they did not see a Black brother but rather a Muslim brother.

To all leaders within the Black Baptist church, it is imperative that we, too, live out our faith in ways that demonstrate Christianity for all humanity, one that is based on our canon and not a created construct. We must positively practice our faith in ways that transform social and congregational views. Robert Banks and Bernice M. Ledbetter state, "Leaders who serve as moral and spiritual exemplars create environments where followers are encouraged to grow in both character and faith, reinforcing the church's witness in the world."[9] Thus, leaders who demonstrate a character akin to Christ and uphold ethical standards have a beneficial impact on the well-being, development, and spiritual growth of their congregations. They contend that leadership grounded in principles of integrity, service, and humility cultivates trust and serves as a model for church members to follow.

We must begin or continue to interact with church members and our communities in ways that inspire them to perceive leaders, the church, and themselves in a new light. I urge the leaders of the local Black Baptist church to adhere to biblical principles that support reconciliation and transformation. I suggest that leaders foster a mindset that encourages social and moral ethics, which can have a positive influence on those in the congregation who are receptive to change. As leaders, we should not be driven by the belief that everyone has already transformed. Instead, we must acknowledge that our Christian responsibility is to uphold a moral and social ethic consistent with our faith tradition.

Dr. Traci C. West, in *Disruptive Christian Ethics: When Racism and Women's Lives Matter*, suggests "to be a valuable resource in this morally competitive climate, a liberatory social ethic based upon the Christian gospel has to be fostered within the concrete

---

8. DeCaro, *On the Side*, loc. 206.
9. Banks, *Reviewing Leadership*, 89.

practices of Christian faith communities."[10] As leaders in Black Baptist churches, we can exemplify our Christian values and inspire others to introspect and discover constructive ways to move ahead. We can take inspiration from Malcolm X's experiences pre-hajj and hajj and aim for conscious interactions that cultivate a positive and distinctive atmosphere among our fellow members. Our conduct can serve as a testament to the unique nature of our community, which is guided by God's wisdom and marked by a difference in behavior.

Given this notion, how might exhibiting our Christianity positively prompt others to perceive something within us that is profoundly unfamiliar, ultimately leading them to view both themselves and us in a fresh light? What strategies can we employ to embody this Christlike nature within our local Black Baptist church to the extent that our communal and interpersonal exchanges serve to assuage years of trauma, mistreatment, disregard, and even self-doubt? Like Malcolm's experiences and encounters with Sunni Muslims, congregational leaders should consistently demonstrate a positive religious ethic that aligns with their faith context. Joe E. Trull and James E. Carter provide background for my assertion. They stated the following:

> The present crisis in ministerial ethics is both a reflection of our times and an influence on our society. Ethical failure in the pulpit affects the pew. At the same time, clergy morals seem to mirror the general decline in morality among the laity. Today's minister walks an ethical tightrope. At one moment, they may serve as a prophet, priest, or educator; in the next, a cleric may be an administrator, a counselor, or a worship leader. Each of these roles raises ethical dilemmas and exposes moral vulnerability not faced by doctors, lawyers, or other professionals.[11]

In evaluating Trull's and Carter's viewpoints, I accept their arguments. While some individuals might hold a different viewpoint, societal transformations influence our understanding of

---

10. West, *Disruptive Christian Ethics*, loc. 126.
11. Trull, *Ministerial Ethics*, 14.

what is deemed ethically right or wrong within congregations. Although there are numerous ethical lapses that are evident and confrontational, shifts in our societal structure have reshaped the perception of what is considered ethical. Pertinent to the experiences of the Black Baptist church is the recognition of ethical standards that are not universally applicable to all Christians but are specific to congregational leaders.

Moreover, as Trull and Carter noted, ethical standards are exclusive rather than inclusive. In our current social climate, who holds greater influence, society or the church? If society has more influence, how can we establish a religious ethic that is unique to our Christian faith, distinct from the ways we operate within congregational or organizational settings? From my perspective, this is the central issue concerning Christian practices and principles within the church, extending beyond just the local Black Baptist church to the global church. Although bi-vocational preachers juggle roles as both pastors and employees, the foundational Christian principles and practices we evaluate should not be solely dictated by the preacher. This idea implies that religious ethics as a practice is entirely the pastor's responsibility due to their role in the congregation, thereby absolving the congregants of their duty to uphold ethical practices.

This notion is harmful to the church. It suggests that individuals who do not serve as congregational leaders or hold ministerial positions are relieved of the obligation to uphold Christian morals, simply because they choose to identify as Christians. Although Trull and Carter do not explicitly state this, it can be inferred. I believe that while congregational leaders should adhere to a moral code of ethics, suggesting that an occupational code of ethics surpasses the ethical standards associated with being a Christian is a significant misrepresentation of our faith context.

Consequently, congregational leaders face challenges in influencing seekers and searchers due to interactions with individuals who profess Christianity as their faith but fail to exhibit an ethic consistent with the Bible, or even the general perception of what it means to be a Christian. Although many perspectives on Christianity from those outside the church are not grounded in sound biblical teachings, a basic understanding of faith implies that we should embody an ethic of love and care. This responsibility does not rest solely on pastors or preachers but on all who identify as Christians.

The role of the Black Baptist pastor in American religious and cultural history has frequently been influenced by racialized sociopolitical contexts, which often obscure the broader application of universal religious ethics. Traditionally, the Black Baptist pastor has served not only as a spiritual guide but also as a sociopolitical figure—championing justice, representing the collective suffering of Black communities, and embodying prophetic resistance. This dual function has led to the perception that Black religious ethics are contextually specific—more reactive than normative—thereby sidelining their contributions to the development of universal religious ethics. This interpretive imbalance stems from the fact that dominant theological and ethical frameworks have historically favored Eurocentric, individualistic, and apolitical approaches to ethical reasoning.

In contrast, the Black pastoral tradition, which is grounded in liberation, communal survival, and social change, is often viewed as particularistic or even exceptional rather than as foundational to universal ethics. Consequently, the moral insights derived from the Black religious experience are frequently regarded as situational ethics rather than as contributions to a comprehensive moral vision for humanity. In her exploration of womanist ethics and theology, Townes tackles this topic head-on. She contends that Black religious figures, particularly female leaders and clergy, have historically contributed significant ethical insights that are frequently overlooked in mainstream ethical discussions. Townes writes, "The ethical insights of African American religious leaders are frequently viewed as responses to oppression rather than as generative of moral universals. This misrepresents both the depth and the scope of Black theological ethics."[12]

---

12. Townes, *Womanist Ethics*, 18.

When No One Leads the Church

RESISTANCE TO THE PROCESS

As an emerging scholar and practitioner in a local Black Baptist church, I am familiar with some of the challenges congregational leaders face. Despite their efforts to align their social ethics with a Christ-centered, Bible-based approach, pastors may still struggle to navigate the transformation process with their congregants. In this section, I will briefly address three modes of resistance to the process. These modes of resistance to the process associated with the Black church are social trauma, a social disposition understood as the "three Fs," and clashes between external development strategies and internal redirection.

Our initial mode of resistance to the process is social trauma. While we know that transformation is possible, what considerations have been taken in assessing the possibilities of transformation in the same space that fostered their trauma? This question is pivotal to the congregational/social leader looking to contribute to the transformational process positively. Archie Smith Jr., in *The Relational Self: Ethics and Therapy from a Black Church Perspective*, asks,

> If the concepts with which we work toward change and the structures of consciousness are formed by the society of which we are apart, then how do we forge alternatives since our own biographies, values, and beliefs are largely determined by the very social processes we hope to change?[13]

Merely shifting our viewpoint is inadequate for addressing congregational or social challenges. For some individuals, the severity of their traumatic experiences necessitates a new environment to explore transformative possibilities. I share this perspective to shed light on the struggles faced by pastors in similar situations, despite their best efforts. Although I am optimistic that my suggestions to congregational leaders will yield positive outcomes, I am aware of the complexities involved in applying them in real-world scenarios.

13. Smith, "Relational Self," 79.

A secondary mode of resistance to the process comes by way of some pastors encountering a social disposition related to a particular ideology of congregational association and behavior I reference as the three Fs: family, friendships, and feelings. This ideology, referred to as the "three Fs," is not linked to traditional doctrines, polities, or governance structures. Instead, it operates within congregational settings as a social disposition manifesting as a reaction to decisions that counter the status quo of FLG members. Often, these decisions affect family ties, friendships, and emotions. Thus, the term: three Fs.

During a recent discussion with a colleague who prefers to remain anonymous, they recounted a tense interaction with a member. In our talk, they mentioned that the member had agreed to a decision, but the actions taken did not reflect that agreement. After the event concluded, my colleague approached the individual to express concerns about the actions that deviated from what was agreed upon. A subsequent meeting was held with several church leaders and my colleague. When the issue was discussed and all details were laid out, most church leaders concurred that the pastor's assessment and communication with the individual were appropriate. However, two leaders pointed out that the individual they had known since childhood could not have said or done what the pastor claimed, despite her admission during the meeting. Due to their close relationship with the individual, viewing her as a friend and family member, they believed the pastor was mistaken because the woman they had watched grow up was deeply hurt. After all, the pastor called her to the proverbial carpet. Her admission of wrongdoing was not considered.

Thirdly, resistance to the process can arise when strategies for external congregational development clash with internal evaluation and redirection efforts within a particular congregation. Matthew Fairholm, in "Leadership and Organizational Strategy," writes,

> We need to comprehend why things operate the way they do and we need to understand that organizational wisdom comes not from programming and prediction, but

rather from an understanding of human motivations, formal and informal organizational values, culture, and inter- and intra-organizational relationships. With a firmer grasp of the Whys of social and organizational interaction, we then can have a clearer picture of what we should, could, can, and cannot do, within those contexts.[14]

As leaders of congregations, it is essential to recognize that what proves effective for one group may not necessarily produce the same outcomes for another. Our duty as leaders is to identify issues within our church and devise strategies that are specifically suited to the distinct characteristics of our members.

Since each congregation is distinct, there is no one-size-fits-all solution for the challenges faced by Black Baptist churches. A leader's role extends beyond delivering sermons to include implementing growth strategies that enable the congregation to reach their full potential without merely replicating other congregations. Given the diversity in membership, social dynamics, financial conditions, and educational levels, it is important to acknowledge and respect these differences. Consequently, the leader's teaching methods should be tailored to the congregation's needs and learning preferences, considering how they process information.

AN AID TO THE PROCESS

As a leader within a congregation, how can one effectively manage the social intricacies present in Black Baptist churches? The essential factor is distinguishing between tension and conflict. Tension is associated with stretching and growth, while conflict, if not properly managed, can lead to rupture or lasting harm. Guiding through tension involves confidently challenging team members' thoughts, attitudes, and emotional reactions, even if it causes discomfort. Although it might not be pleasant, tension is crucial for sustained growth and development. In a previous instance, my

---

14. Fairholm, "Leadership and Organizational Strategy," 6.

colleague chose not to persuade two leaders who were unable to recognize the truth for their own sake. Instead, other leaders who had built relationships with these two individuals took the time to express what the pastor felt but what the two leaders did not accept. This leadership concept is known as the 25-50-25 rule.

According to John Maxwell, there exists a leadership principle known as the 25-50-25 rule. Essentially, this rule suggests that 25 percent of your congregation will never change and will resist any attempts to appease them. On the other hand, 25 percent of your congregation will support your ministry efforts with enthusiasm and joy. These members will embrace your vision and follow where God is leading you. The remaining 50 percent are undecided and may need encouragement to sway their opinion. In essence, this principle highlights the importance of giving credibility to the 25 percent who support you, as they can influence the 50 percent of undecided members. By working with them, you can effectively move the organization forward.[15]

A shared comprehension of mutuality serves as an additional support in guiding leaders and congregants toward correct beliefs and behaviors. To grasp my perspective, I examine mutuality through the lens of interdependence theory. This theory is defined as "an approach to analyzing social interactions and relationships that focuses on how each person's outcomes depend on the actions of others."[16] Therefore, my view of mutuality as interpreted through interdependence theory, implies that in environments where the development of mutuality is deliberate, "partners depend equally on each other's behavior for the attainment of desirable outcomes."[17] A mutual dependence on behaviors suggests that belief alone offers an incomplete demonstration of what is needed to establish congregational mutuality. Ethics in this context must be intentionally practiced in ways that seek to bring the church to the place that best represents who they collectively wish to become.

---

15. Maxwell, "25-50-25 Principle of Change."
16. *APA Dictionary of Psychology*, "Interdependence Theory."
17. *APA Dictionary of Psychology*, "Mutuality."

Sharon Galgay Ketcham, professor of theology and Christian ministries at Gordon College in Massachusetts, suggests that "a theology of mutuality that offers shared experiences, activities, and relationships that involve each person's agency could be transformative but requires the Church to unite diverse gifts and differing wills for the purpose of ministry."[18] The idea of congregational mutuality should be a primary objective for the ministry that both the congregational leader and members of the reformed or future reformed family legacy group should adopt. A unified message, articulated by everyone striving for mutuality and transformation, needs to emerge as a cohesive proclamation from both the pulpit and the pew, serving as a link for congregational mutuality. Achieving congregational mutuality is not necessary to promote the notion that it is possible. Only self-reflection and faith are needed to set the pendulum in motion. In examining the life experiences of Malcolm X as a model for the Black Baptist church, I will cite Louis A. DeCaro Jr.'s complete quote from his book *On the Side of My People* to substantiate my argument. According to DeCaro,

> Apart from his own personal reevaluation of the white race and his euphoria over the spiritual kinship of the Hajj, Malcolm's letters to the press made clear his belief both in the possibility and even the necessity of a religiously guided racial reconciliation in the United States. "The immediate acceptance of the oneness of God," preached Malcolm, "is the only way out, the only way America can escape the inevitable destruction that every racist nation brings upon itself when it becomes too intoxicated with its power to recognize the existence of a Spiritual Power greater than all of its military and nuclear might." By recognizing the "Spiritual Power" of Allah, Malcolm contended, whites in the United States could redeem both themselves and their nation because an embrace of the oneness of God would guarantee their acceptance of the oneness of man. "America" could be spared the destruction of "the cancer of racism" by

---

18. Flynt, "Theology of Mutuality."

becoming acquainted with Islam, "a religion that has molded people of all colors into one vast family.[19]

While I don't share Malcolm's view of Sunni Islam as the only path to reshaping society, I do believe that religion, in all its forms, can shape our social beliefs and ethics and influence how we engage with one another.

For some Black Baptist churches, congregational mutuality can potentially exist as the foundation of communal equality and congregational equity. To overcome the issues of control and power that can hinder congregations, we need to establish a plan that encourages shared goals, accountability, and responsibility for all members. The congregation can make significant progress by transitioning to a model of collective leadership, fellowship, and optimal functionality. While controversial for some, leaders within the Black Baptist church can observe and assess the behavioral practices of Sunni Muslims in the East as a positive example of ethical practices contributing to social engagement. The unique social behavior demonstrated in their daily faith practice aligns with their traditional beliefs. The objective of this assessment is not to integrate Islamic practices into Christian congregational spaces but rather to investigate social ethics and human behaviors in ways that positively contribute to healthy behavioral practices of Black Baptist church leaders. This information may encourage the implementation of consistent moral and human behaviors that align with the tenets of our faith context. By examining Malcolm X's experiences and encounters in Jeddah and Mecca, we can better understand how this hypothesis would manifest in practical application.

CONCLUSION

Malcolm's experiences in Mecca offer valuable insights into the behavioral and ethical dynamics that we, as leaders of the Black Baptist church, can implement in our interactions with all congregation

---

19. DeCaro, *On the Side*, loc. 208–9.

members, regardless of race, education, class, or preference. I want to clarify that I am not suggesting that we adopt Islamic faith practices but instead that we strive to make our Christian faith practices just as impactful to those we encounter. Malcolm serves as an archetype for members of the Black Baptist church, reminding us that our actions and beliefs have the potential to transform the lives of those around us radically. By living out our faith in positive and proactive ways, we can contribute to our church community's holistic redevelopment and transformation of the Malcolms in our church and community.

In examining mutuality as an extension of transformation within the local Black Baptist church, jointly assessing the actions and behaviors of FLG members and leaders is crucial to the process. Thus, both groups must establish a shared understanding as the foundation for mutuality. While focusing on reshaping FLG members, I also recognize the importance of positive, sustained human and social behavior from leaders in the Black Baptist church. These positive, sustained behaviors contribute to a healthy social environment. We must critically evaluate methodology and intentionality in our practices to ensure the long-term sustainability of congregational transformation through mutuality in the Black Baptist church.

To achieve optimal outcomes, I think it is essential for Black Baptist/Black congregational leaders to engage in self-reflection to understand the underlying reasons that shape their beliefs and actions. After experiencing a form of liturgical hazing, clergy in Black churches endure a systemic harshness imposed by those they serve. Although the ethical implications of these practices have never been addressed, it is crucial to emphasize the impact of these social and congregational traditions that are systematically passed down to each new generation of leaders. This perpetuation of negative ethics continues to contribute to clergy trauma. When these issues are raised by the current generation of preachers, experienced clergy often fail to recognize the harm caused by these practices. Instead, they view the younger clergy as lacking strength and readiness for the challenges of ministry. To disrupt the cycle of trauma within our churches, change must begin at the top and permeate throughout the entire community. When appropriately executed, leaders of Black Baptist churches can witness incredible transformations and the cultivation of mutual respect and understanding from those who engage in the process.

CHAPTER 5

Lent and Pilgrimage: Congregational Practices that Lead to Transformation

WITHIN THE RICH SPIRITUAL heritage of the Black Baptist church, practices like Lent and pilgrimage possess a transformative influence, serving not just as liturgical rituals but as collective disciplines that resonate with the spirit of a community shaped by adversity, resilience, and hope. Lent, with its focus on fasting, prayer, and repentance, mirrors the Black church's historical emphasis on moral clarity, social justice, and spiritual renewal. It encourages congregations to challenge oppressive systems, both internally and externally, guiding them toward the liberating grace of God through introspection and disciplined action.

Similarly, the concept of pilgrimage, whether it involves actual travels to holy sites or represents metaphorical journeys toward spiritual and communal freedom, holds significant meaning within the Black Baptist church's enduring view of faith as a voyage. From the harrowing experiences of the Middle Passage to the mass relocations of the Great Migration, and from civil rights marches to spiritual searches for identity and belonging, pilgrimage in the Black religious imagination often acts as both a lament and a testament, highlighting God's presence during times of movement, change, and transformation.

Lent and pilgrimage together present the Black Baptist church with significant frameworks for revitalizing congregations.

They offer organized chances to reflect, resist, and envision life in Christ, deeply embedded in the narratives, music, and sacred customs of those who have long discovered ways to endure and flourish in faith. This section of the book will examine how these traditions serve as tools for spiritual transformation within Black congregational life, connecting ancient Christian practices with the ongoing experiences of a community persistently moving toward freedom.

THE HISTORY OF LENT

In delving into the history of Lent, we uncover deep personal ties. The way Lent is interpreted and understood has changed over time. Initially, in the East, Lent was a specific period for new believers to fast as they prepared for baptism. Easter, a crucial event in the Christian church, celebrated Jesus' resurrection and represented fresh starts for both believers and the church. Lent also offered a chance for those who had distanced themselves from the church to contemplate and renew their commitment to God and the church. This personal link to Lent's history, along with the challenges and victories of our faith ancestors, is more than just a historical fact; it is an active, vibrant part of our spiritual journey. It serves as a powerful means to enhance our understanding and appreciation of this sacred time.

Although those who practiced Lent during the early part of its formation from the East engaged in previously addressed practices, Lent took on a different form of interpretation and interest as a practice in the West. Russo asserts,

> In the West, on the other hand, the ritual markers that would come to distinguish it from the rest of Lent— e.g., the unveiling of the statues and the singing of the *Gloria* on Maundy Thursday—emerge too late to tell us anything about the relationship between the two periods earlier in history.[1]

---

1. Russo, "Early History of Lent," 20.

After the development of Lent as a fixed forty-day event, Lent's focus did not associate itself with themes related to Lent's origin story from the East. Lent in the West was not a preparatory period for new converts or returning believers. Instead, Lent was a liturgical practice for individuals already connected to the Christian church. As a liturgical practice, Lent spoke to repentance, soul searching, sorrow for sin, and ascetical disciplines of self-denial. This universal nature of Lent, practiced in various forms across the Christian world, unites us in our shared devotion and commitment while highlighting our faith's diverse interpretations and practices.[2]

There are several primary Lenten practices in today's churches. These practices comprise the Lenten themes: repentance, forgiveness, prayer, reflection, fasting, and sacrifice. When implemented, these Lenten practices can produce renewal and transformation.[3] During the practices of repentance and forgiveness, those who engage in this stage step into the realm of self-evaluation, assessing their choices and practices antithetical to that which pleases God and seeks the forgiveness only God provides. Prayer and reflection offer space to talk with God and reflect on ways to better oneself. My interpretation of bettering speaks to steps encouraging introspection, spiritual development, and fostering spaces deepening our relationship with God.

LENTEN PRACTICES AND ITS ASSOCIATION TO TRANSFORMATION

The practices of fasting and sacrifice address the importance of self-denial and spiritual discipline. Both fasting and sacrifice connect those who engage in these practices with the concept of suffering. Fasting is the deliberate act of surrendering creature comforts to renounce distractions that deter us from focusing on God's plans and purpose for our lives, and fasting and sacrificing

---

2. Hunter, "Preaching Lent," 10.
3. Kearney, "4 Themes of Lent," 1–6.

foster focus. They allow those who engage in them to see what is essential. It highlights the significance of humility, gratitude, and consideration for others. If the themes of sacrifice/self-denial and repentance relating to Lenten practices contribute to reshaping members of the Black Baptist church, FLG members, in particular, must step away from normative behaviors and practices in their social and congregational spaces and seek to embrace Lenten practices.

When embraced without resistance or restraint, members of the congregation can assess Lent's interpretation of self-denial and soul searching as a spiritual discipline to reshape. If I posit that FLG members subscribe to a created perspective that offers a varying understanding of how the local Black Baptist church should function, giving something up as a Lenten practice can be a transformative aid. Although Lent does not serve as a supportive companion to materialistic practices of American society, Lent, by interpretation, is a time of self-denial and pondering the mystery of suffering; a time of self-abasement; a time for doing without, purging and cleansing, for purification.[4] When taught and practiced correctly, Lent can be a powerful tool in the reshaping process. Through the teaching of self-denial and the implementation of ritual practices, FLG members can engage in personal and corporate prayer gatherings, meditation, and topic-specific textual readings that encourage redevelopment. Lent and its tenets of sacrifice, death, and rebirth can function as a catalyst for transformation. This stage operates as the "bridging" stage in the transformation process. As a launching formation, the congregation and the community can begin developing a new fundamental belief, actualized in a modified behavior that transforms the congregation.

Can introducing self-denial create a lasting impact? One would hope that it would, but several variables must be considered to provide a suitable answer to this question. In referencing the Wayside Baptist Church specifically, tensions are present in this congregational space between the current pastor and several members of the family legacy group. Although the information

4. Hunter, "Preaching Lent," 10.

that the pastor and the teaching staff wish to provide is essential for their growth and development, hesitation to embrace and accept this information is present within their social context.

Suppose some barriers impede the connection between the new pastor, the teaching staff, and influential members of the family legacy group. In that case, everything and everyone associated with the new congregational leader and their staff is scrutinized. What then must happen to reclaim a working space of community so that openness can occur and the tenets of Lent are embraced? In referencing teacher–student relations, Hans Créton, Theo Wubbels, and Herman Hooymayers elaborate on a shared perspective that informs the instructor/teacher on the solutions and potential barriers that impact cooperative communication between teacher and student in each learning environment, depicted as circularity and change. They write,

> The concepts of circularity and change are central to an understanding of systems theory and help describe all other characteristics. Circularity implies that all aspects of a system are intertwined. Changes in one will not only affect the others but will then return like ripples of water moving between banks. Thus, circular communication processes develop that not only consist of behavior but also determine behavior. The nature of any system, then, is greatly affected by its response—and, in some cases, resistance—to change.[5]

While seldom discussed in congregational spaces, social systems/theory is active within the church. Thus, when evaluated and practiced, the congregational leader and their teaching staff can implement strategies associated with social theory/systems in the church, create strategies that help to break down social barriers in the congregation, and present information that is absorbable to all who participate as learners within the congregation.

---

5. Créton, "Systems Perspective," 1–2.

Lent & Pilgrimage

AN EXPANDED INTERPRETATION OF LENTEN PRACTICES

In some instances, the forty-day Lenten season does not offer adequate time to significantly impact the lives of individuals new to faith practices or those needing transformation. Therefore, I propose a new interpretation of Lent that posits it as a lifestyle practice, extending beyond the Lenten season. Through the ongoing practice of self-denial, congregants can reshape ideals and behaviors that hinder the possibility of survival mode relapse. Lent creates a space for individuals to self-reflect and reevaluate what matters. Through this reevaluation process, FLG members can reassess the sacrifices of the historical Jesus and what they are willing to give up for Jesus Christ. This teaching component must make Christ the focal point, not the church or the concept of reshaping. Reshaping must be a voluntary act of the FLG member whose connection to Christ motivates them to reassess ideas and ideals that do not align with a mission of reconciliation and transformation.

As previously stated, the mission of Jesus grounds itself on the actions of reconciliation and transformation. This mission is the fundamental, established interpretation of how the Black Baptist church must govern itself. Thus, when teaching the principles of self-denial during the Lenten season, individuals in the congregation can rethink how they interpret mission, ministry, social engagement, and congregational governance. During this period of Lent, members in the congregation can create prayer partners, develop topic-specific reading assignments, and foster personal and collective spaces of meditation and self-reflection.

For family legacy group members in the local Black Baptist church, I posit a reimagining of Lent lived out through the concept of Lent as a lifestyle. Lent, for some, must expand its practices beyond a short-lived season. Due to limitations associated with methods needed to foster redevelopment and transformation, challenges with congregational sustainability in specific perspectives exist. While the leadership of the local Black Baptist church desires to see the Black Baptist church reshaped and transformed, often we do not invest enough time and patience for congregants to go through the process needed to redevelop a new perspective—a new ideal of congregational understanding and behavior. We must be intentional and consistent in our teaching strategy for Lent. While some will latch on and forge ahead, for others, it may take some time to "lay aside the weight and the sin that clings so closely."[6]

PILGRIMAGE AS A PRACTICE

I assert that pilgrimage serves as a transformational practice that can contribute to the deconstruction of survival mode dynamics. What is a pilgrimage? George D. Greenia, in his 2018 article in the *International Journal of Religious Tourism and Pilgrimage* entitled, "What Is Pilgrimage?" offers a working interpretation of the term that will ground our understanding and use of the term in this section of the book. Greenia writes, "The term 'pilgrimage' has become commonplace in modern conversations about any travel announced as 'intentional,' 'purposeful,' 'transformative,' or simply promises to be 'authentic.'"[7] Thus, the tenets of our understanding of pilgrimage recognize pilgrimage as a journey grounded in purpose that transforms the lives of those participating in its practice. While practiced historically amongst people classed as tribal, over time, mainline religions embraced pilgrimage as a practice and associated it with an institutional tenet.

In assessing the lived experiences and encounters of Malcolm X as my example of journeying from transition to transformation, I posit that pilgrimage is a necessary step that leads to change. The Muslim pilgrimage differs from other religions that engage in the pilgrimage experience. Hajj is one of five pillars of faith for Muslims, making pilgrimage a religious duty owed to God. All Muslims of sound mind and health who are financially able to make the time for hajj are encouraged to go. Additionally, the practice of hajj is supported by the Holy Quran. Martin asserts, "Hajj symbolism

6. Heb 12:1, NIV.
7. Greenia, *What Is Pilgrimage*, 7.

carries overtones of ancient Arab and Judeo-Christian cosmologies, which resonate in the appointed times and places of the ritual performances."[8] Unique to the hajj experience is the social and religious unity of the pilgrimage. This sacred gathering temporarily engages individuals of varying ethnicities, languages, and social classes. Social status is substituted for mutuality and brotherhood for all people. Thus, the hajj experience not only differs from other religious pilgrimage encounters but also differs from the teachings of the Nation of Islam.

Malcolm's transformation would not have been as impactful apart from his pilgrimage. One would assume that Malcolm's pilgrimage began in Mecca, but I would suggest that Malcolm's pilgrimage started much earlier. Since pilgrimage as a practice functions as a form of a rite of passage, Malcolm's example of pilgrimage displays itself through three stages: instruction of traditional Islam, his journey to Mecca, and his return to the States. Thus, Malcolm's encounters with Ahmed Osman and Dr. Shawarbi (the start of pilgrimage), his travels to the holy city of Mecca (the journey of pilgrimage), and his transformation and return to America (the conclusion of pilgrimage) served as a conduit used to transport him between the stages of where he once was to who he would ultimately become.

Heather A. Warfield, in "Quest for Transformation: An Exploration of Pilgrimage in the Counseling Process," writes,

> The desire of humans to connect with an element of the sacred is evident from the writings of our distant ancestors to modern publications. This desire has manifested itself through rites of passage, rituals, and structures dedicated to the object of one's veneration. Often, the site of the physical structure or area of land evolves into a meaningful connection point with the sacred or divine. As such, once the site has been identified as this connection point, individuals or groups continue to visit the site through a journey identified as a pilgrimage.[9]

---

8. Martin, "Pilgrimage," 1.
9. Warfield, "Quest for Transformation," 1.

Based on Warfield's assertion, pilgrimage, apart from a connection to sacredness, does not offer a realistic interpretation of a whole pilgrimage experience. To the Black church member, our association or, better yet, our connection to symbolism contrasts Islamic symbolism and other Christian-based religious denominations' symbolism for one primary reason. Most Black churches are autonomous. As an autonomous body, certain Black Baptist churches do not directly associate themselves with what we historically understand as creeds and liturgy. Often, religious symbolism is an extension of created creeds and liturgy connected to a particular faith or denominational context. Thus, we see symbolism actively displayed in Catholic, Lutheran, and Orthodox churches worldwide but not similarly in Black churches. Even the terminology in several Black Baptist churches is exclusive to that particular church. The two observed practices in the church, communion and baptism, are termed ordinances instead of sacraments.

Often, pilgrimage associates its practice with some form of symbolism. The concept of journeying is universal in its interpretation, but typically, no faith context speaks of pilgrimage apart from an associated shrine or symbol of significance. As Protestant participants of the Christian church, some of our sister Protestant churches embrace symbols in the forms of shrines, statues, and pictures as reference points. This medium is often excluded in the Black church. We then are left to exercise pilgrimage practices not through symbolism but rather through the lens of journeying.

PILGRIMAGE FROM A DIFFERENT LENS

The implications of pilgrimage in the context that I wish to present as a practice applicable for FLG members in the local Black Baptist church seeks to expand the traditional concept of pilgrimage. My theory posits an additional perspective of pilgrimage that includes an understanding of pilgrimage as a journey of the mind. This mind journey contributes to reshaping what we believe and how we behave. Although the sacredness of pilgrimage "can be defined in terms of physical, psychological, emotional, social, and spiritual constructs,"[10] we do not have to limit the practice to physical journeying exclusively.

Although physical leave-taking is the customary form of pilgrimaging, I wish to offer a broader lens by which we can interpret the concept of pilgrimage. My theory on pilgrimage does not maximize pilgrimage as a practice to a traditional sense of physical leave-taking. Instead, it offers an augmented lens that incorporates mental, emotional, and psychological leave-taking as an option. Looking at pilgrimage through this lens allows individuals to experience pilgrimage as a practice beyond its original designation of physical traveling. Let us look at meditation as a reference to a pilgrimage practice that does not involve leave-taking.

Meditation, also understood as mindfulness methods, is a practice that involves focusing one's attention on the present moment, cultivating awareness and acceptance of thoughts, emotions, and physical sensations without judgment. It transports our minds to other places, even though our physical bodies have not moved. Meditation has parallels to indigenous cultural practices. Some of these practices trace back to Native American and Hindu spiritual rituals. Native American ritual is considered a shamanic tradition. While shamanic practices involve a spiritual guide in their ritual performance, the meditative practice for the participant presents a "pathless path from here to here."[11] Thus, journeying in this concept is not physical. My reference to this practice seeks to offer parallels to my thoughts around pilgrimage that do not involve physical travel.

In *Cyberpilgrimage: The (Virtual) Reality of Online Pilgrimage Experience*, Connie Hill-Smith associates a similar theory of non-travel pilgrimage, which contrasts the traditional concept of leave-taking. Smith writes,

> Cyberpilgrimage is the practice of undertaking pilgrimage on the internet. Such pilgrimages may be performed for a host of reasons, ranging from idle curiosity to the need to ready oneself, psychologically or informationally,

---

10. Warfield, "Therapeutic Value of Pilgrimage," 860–75.
11. Tollifson, *Nothing to Grasp*, 12.

for a "real" (terrestrial) pilgrimage. Depending on individual motivations and circumstances, however, they can be deeply charged, transformative, enlightening, and profoundly fulfilling on both emotional and spiritual levels.[12]

Although virtual pilgrimage in some arenas is comparable to meditative pilgrimage, critics assess this form skeptically. Questions around authenticity and depth of experience raise issues in certain academic circles.

I reference mental trekking as an additional interpretation of my theory. This premise can transcend our minds and teleport us into another space. Kathryn M. Rudy, in "A Guide to Mental Pilgrimage: Paris, Bibliothèque de L'Arsenal Ms. 212," posits this concept as a "mental or virtual pilgrimage." While Rudy shares my premise of mental trekking, her use of the idea also uses symbols and manuscripts as a supportive tool of mental pilgrimage. She writes,

> Arsenal 212 is a manuscript with text and images that evoke the Church of the Holy Sepulcher in Jerusalem and provides prayers to be read in praise of the Temple of the Lord according to the rubric (fol.2). The corresponding image depicts the church's exterior. The manuscript then provides prayers and closely related miniatures evoking chapels within the Church of the Holy Sepulcher: the Chapel of the Virgin Mary, the Chapel of the Magdalen, the Chapel of the Flagellation, and the chapel marking the place where the soldiers divided Christ's robe.[13]

Although a manuscript specific to pilgrimage for FLG members in the local Black Baptist church does not exist, I believe several topical books on prayer, meditation, and journeys would be theologically appropriate as a companion tool for pilgrimaging in place. Thus, any space can become sacred, where we can center ourselves and connect with the divine. When pilgrimage through mental leave-taking creates a different construct, we can utilize this new

---

12. Hill-Smith, "Cyberpilgrimage," 236–46.
13. Rudy, "Guide to Mental Pilgrimage," 494–515.

construction to reshape the social constructs that historically informed our cultural, social, and religious identity in ways that previously were antithetical to God's original design for the local Black Baptist church.

Relating to the experiences of Malcolm X, whereas hajj (pilgrimage) is considered a requirement of the Islamic faith, leave-taking does not have to be the only practice for the FLG member who engages in this practice. What we must embrace are ways to encourage the need for pilgrimage as a necessity in the local Black church. By associating pilgrimage with Christian faith practices, we can connect what we already do, i.e., prayer, meditation, exercise, and the like, and use our faith practices as a participating partner in our expression of journeying. This concept came to me because of COVID-19 a few years ago. Let us take a moment to look at this concept through customary church-based practices impacted by COVID.

While participating in retreats has served as a means of pilgrimage in the past for members of the local Black church, our most recent experiences with COVID-19 and our nationwide isolation during that time suggested that the concept of retreat must expand itself beyond the practice of leave-taking. Thus, what we claim as a designated point or location of a pilgrimage can no longer exist in ways that present pilgrimage as a disconnection from our current physical site. Instead, we must employ other options that foster a similar sense without vacating. While the world is progressively returning to a sense of normalcy, the church has not yet fully recovered from the effects of COVID. Thus, the church must develop means of ministry that expand our customary scope.

SACRED SPACE

How does one denote a space as sacred? What factors must we consider when authenticating a specific location as sacred? We often see buildings erected with various religious symbols on them. Whether Jewish synagogues, Catholic cathedrals, mosques, or regular Protestant church buildings, these buildings, for most, are considered sacred. In reflecting on our understanding of sacred space in contemporary discourse, we may need to broaden our scope of sacred spaces. For instance, church-plant ministries of varying Protestant denominational affiliations are reconditioning our perceptions regarding sacred space. The contemporary church no longer limits the sacred space to a traditional church building. Banquet halls, gymnasiums, school auditoriums, movie theatres, and even bars are meeting spaces for religious gatherings. The cornerstone of interpreting what is sacred is based on the people, not the location.

Relating to our Christian understanding, the church, regardless of denominational affiliation or Christian identity marker, is interpreted as the ecclesia, the "called-out ones." Thus, sacred space should not be defined exclusively by physical buildings that hold religious sentimental value. Instead, sacredness should be determined by the individuals who live out their faith context in whatever space they choose to gather. This understanding suggests that a new interpretation of sacred space is necessary. Congregational landscapes are no longer centralized to buildings and erected cathedrals. Congregational landscapes are also cyber sites and Zoom rooms.

While many of our traditional congregational spaces still exist and several members still attend in person, many congregants are beginning to frequent the fixed location as they did in the past. Considering the impacts of COVID-19 on our world in general and the local Black church in particular, how do we reinterpret congregational landscapes in today's climate? What serves as markers that determine how we consider sacred space? Most of our local Black churches have had to readjust how they function. Wang asserts that "religious attendance has declined significantly in the past two years. The share of regular churchgoers is down by six percentage points, from 34% in 2019 to 28% in 2021."[14]

Elizabeth Hoffman Ransford offers her view of a historical interpretation of sacred spaces on religious landscapes in her Loyola University Chicago dissertation entitled "Sacred Spaces, Public

---

14. Wang, "Decline in Church Attendance," 4.

Places: The Intersection of Religion and Space in Three Chicago Communities, 1869–1932." She writes,

> As the most tangible displays of religion on the landscape, religious structures embody and shape believers' theological understandings, cultural assumptions, and social aspirations; sacred buildings convey how congregations perceive themselves and how they aspire to be perceived by others. Moreover, because houses of worship serve as visible markers of the cultural authority and political status of their builders, religious structures also reflect the secular values and aesthetic fashions of the public sphere.[15]

Family legacy group members may need to reassess how they think about congregational governance since the church's landscape has changed. While I do not seek to appear insensitive to the myriads of families who have experienced loss over the last several years due to COVID-19, I wish to posit a reassessment of COVID-19 in ways that offer a different lens of interpretation. Could COVID-19 be perceived as an act of divine disconnection? What if the church no longer demonstrated a lens of Christianity that mirrors God's intended design for God's church; could COVID-19, during its original entrance to our geographical landscape, exist as a religious/congregational break? If so, how do we reimagine sacred space? How do we reassess journeying? As previously inferred, sacred space can no longer exist as a representation of concrete buildings alone. Sacred space must be a visual depiction of a gathering expanse created by people who live consecrated lives. Thus, consecrated people transform ordinary spaces into an expanse of the sacred.

Let us reference one of Moses' experiences to substantiate my premise. Moses is living in Midian with his wife, Zipporah, tending to the sheep of his father-in-law, Jethro. While leading his flock, Moses makes his way through Mt. Horeb. While referenced as the mountain of God, this mountain served as a daily trail that Moses used to herd his sheep. On one occasion, Moses notices a

---

15. Ransford, "Sacred Spaces, Public Places," 1–2.

burning bush on the mountain that the fire has not consumed. While investigating this strange occurrence, Moses hears his name called twice from the fire. God told Moses to remove his sandals, for the terrain he currently stood on is now sacred ground.

Based on this encounter, this mountain section is temporarily perceived as consecrated territory via the presence of the divine, whose power projects itself through a selected object on the mountain, seen as fire. Now deemed sacred, this terrain is the same region where Moses often led his flock. Before this encounter, this area was a section of the mountain covered with trees and bushes. Still, the presence of one who is holy transformed this region into a consecrated domain, making it more than what it had been previously. In reading the biblical narrative from which the story emanates, there is no reference to a continued state of sacredness beyond this dialogue between God and Moses between Exod 3–4.

What we witness in this context is a place centered by person-centered sacredness.[16] This theory suggests that individuals are the carriers of sacredness. Thus, wherever carriers of holiness find themselves, sacredness accompanies them. With this understanding at the heart of our premise of reimagining sacred space, I posit that consecrated spaces are only as credible as their association with those deemed consecrated. While the representation of God in the Exodus narrative does not minimize God to a human-based description, I reference the term "person" as a generic term to substantiate my claim.

The members of the local Black church must reimagine how we understand sacred space by reassessing what represents sacredness. Our reassessment of sacredness must become a preamble that includes those who make up the power dynamic in the church. Thus, sacredness can no longer exist as something taught by some. Instead, it must exist as something lived out by all. Unique to my perspective are the experiences and encounters of Malcolm X.

Malcolm encountered sacredness firsthand during his transitional period and week in the Holy Land of Mecca. Had his newfound introduction to the hermeneutics of traditional Islam not

---

16. Eade, *Contesting the Sacred*, 7.

been met with an aligned ethic through his social interaction, traditional Islam would have been nothing more than good reading instead of life-changing. As those who fostered an aligned ethic similar to a transformative perspective in Malcolm's life encounters, we must ensure that sacredness grounds our sacred space regardless of our roles in the congregational arena. This interpretation suggests we must be doers of the word and not only hearers.[17]

OPEN TO LEARNING

Like Malcolm, family legacy group members must develop an appetite for learning that catalyzes pilgrimage. For Malcolm, understanding his traditional faith context grounded his transformation due to his ousting from the NOI. Malcolm's break from the Nation of Islam provided the opportunity needed to develop new associations and learning partnerships. This experience and premise might challenge FLG members easily influenced by family dynamics. "Family dynamics" refers to the patterns of interactions among relatives, their roles and relationships, and the various factors that shape their interactions. Because family members rely on each other for emotional, physical, and economic support, they are one of the primary sources of relationship security or stress.[18]

Specific to family legacy group members of the Wayside Baptist Church, their congregational connection extends their bloodline association. Thus, the opportunity for openness related to new associations and new ways of interpreting how things should be done according to an established understanding of polity may be problematic. It all depends on who exists as the voice of influence within the family legacy group and who in the group is open to varying interpretations, if for nothing else but a comparison tool. In "Constructing Reality and Its Alternatives: An Inclusion/Exclusion Model of Assimilation and Contrast Effects in Social Judgment," Norbert Schwarz and Herbert Bless support my claim. They write,

17. Jas 1:22, NIV.
18. Hunter, "Preaching Lent," 10.

Individuals do not retrieve all knowledge that may bear on the stimulus, nor do they retrieve and use all knowledge that may potentially be relevant to constructing its alternative. Instead, they rely on the subset of potentially relevant information that is most accessible at the time of judgment. Accordingly, their temporary representation of the target stimulus, as well as their construction of a standard of comparison, includes information that is chronically accessible and, hence, context-independent, as well as information that is only temporarily accessible due to contextual influences.[19]

Referencing Malcolm X, family legacy group members who want to undergo the reshaping process must discover ways to establish mental freedom while remaining in congregational proximity to FLG members who wish to maintain the status quo. Malcolm's independence from the Honorable Elijah Muhammad and the Nation of Islam allowed him to deepen his knowledge of Sunni Islam.[20] Family legacy group members desiring redevelopment still associate themselves with the church group who live out their survival modalities. Even if they opt to remain in their domiciles as an act of disassociation from other members of the family legacy group, it does not change the fact that they exist as bloodline associates. Our only hope is that the practice of sacrifice, seen in the spiritual discipline of self-denial, can contribute to ways family legacy group members see Jesus and ultimately see themselves.

---

19. Schwarz, "Constructing Reality," 218.
20. DeCaro, *On the Side*, 202.

CHAPTER 6

Transforming

TRANSFORMATION IS AN ESSENTIAL and evolving process that touches the essence of human development on both personal and collective levels. It presents opportunities for renewal, healing, and reorientation, encouraging individuals and communities to transcend stagnation, brokenness, or constraints, and to achieve a deeper understanding of purpose and identity. In spiritual and moral realms, transformation goes beyond mere behavioral change, representing a profound shift in perception, values, and direction. It enables a reimagining of one's relationship with God, oneself, and others, paving the way toward wholeness, justice, and liberation. Thus, transformation is not only beneficial but also crucial for those pursuing meaningful and lasting change.

What I propose as the process of transformation or its various stages, as reflected in Malcolm X's personal experiences and interactions, parallels the phases of a pilgrimage useful to those in the Black church. Using this perspective as my foundation, I will refer to the pilgrimage stages in this chapter to interpret transformation as a process. If transformation as a process is effective, those who participate must recognize the significance of the movement. No one or nothing seeking transformation can engage in this process without any form of movement. Movement, also understood as mobilities research, stresses several essential aspects of this emerging field of study, including the inter-relational dynamics between physical, informational, virtual, and imaginative forms of mobility, which connects to my premise.[1] Therefore, how one moves does not negate the significance of movement/mobility as an active participant in the transforming process.

In her work *Transformative Experience*, L. A. Paul introduces a novel theory: You can have an experience that is so unlike previous experiences you have had that, before you have the new experience, you cannot know what it is going to be like for you to have it.[2] This theory suggests that we do not consciously anticipate the magnitude of our future encounters and experiences. It is not about potentiality, hopes, or possibilities but about the impact of new experiences that we evaluate the significance of the encounter post-experience. While not all new experiences lead to positive outcomes, I focus on how our new experiences can transform us personally. Therefore, a post-encounter evaluation of lived experiences underscores the role of movement in transformation. This idea serves as a framework for understanding the significance of Malcolm's and reformed FLG members' transformation.

To fully grasp my perspective on transformation, let's delve into the stages of pilgrimage, which I view as a model for interpretation. The transformation process, like the stages of pilgrimage, involves separation/detachment, liminality, and reintegration. In most cases, separation/detachment serves as the initiation stage. All participants in the transformation process experience some form of separation/detachment. This stage can be forced, embraced, or even traumatic. Let us examine these stages in more detail.

THE PROCESS—SEPARATION/DETACHMENT

In each analysis, transformation commences with detachment. Detachment is crucial, as it creates a space for learning free from the influence of heretical systems of understanding and social control. Detachment provides space for social and cognitive

1. Collins-Kreiner, "Researching Pilgrimage," 44056.
2. Paul, *Transformative Experience*, 5.

disconnections. Over time, separation can reconstruct previously constructed theories that are the foundation of our knowledge and ethics—individuals who genuinely desire growth and expansion of thought present opportunities for critical thinking and investigation. T. Merton asserts, "Detachment is not the denial of desire but the denial of the possession and control of desire. True transformation requires a letting go—not only of external things, but also of the ego's need to cling to self-image, status, or security."[3] Although Malcolm's and the reformed FLG members' experiences regarding detachment differ, their similarities provide context for the importance of separation as a catalyst for transformation. Consequently, detachment becomes crucial in bolstering my comprehension of the transformational process. While detachment may not be linked directly to what I previously referred to as a sacred space, it serves as a necessary step in fostering a new epistemology.

Transformation of beliefs and attitudes requires exposure to new information and understanding its significance. Some social and religious contexts are particularly resistant to change, as long-standing traditions and beliefs often shape them. However, when new information and separation are introduced, it is essential to evaluate its implications and how they align with our current understanding. Unfortunately, this process is often hindered by the repetition of familiar ideas and the influence of those in power, reinforcing their existing beliefs and preventing transformation—hence, the significance of detaching. We need to actively pursue new knowledge and participate in open dialogues to challenge existing ideas. By exploring various perspectives and considering different viewpoints, we can expand our understanding and reassess our beliefs. The experiences of individuals like Malcolm X and the transformed members of the family legacy group offer valuable insights into how new information can influence personal and societal development. Acknowledging the significance of lifelong learning and being receptive to new concepts, even if they contradict current beliefs, is essential. Let us delve into the cases of Malcolm X and the reformed FLG members.

3. Merton, *New Seeds of Contemplation*, 21.

In both instances, they were deeply embedded in a social and cognitive framework that influential individuals had a hand in shaping. These individuals wielded significant influence over their loyalty and devotion. Malcolm X, the truth-seeker, framed his acceptance of truth as what aligned with the teachings of the Honorable Elijah Muhammad. Malcolm did not present his messages exclusively around the principles of the Quran. Instead, he sought to please Elijah based on his reverence for him. Hence, his public speeches consistently referenced the Honorable Elijah Muhammad's words. For Malcolm, separation from the NOI and the ideology of Muhammed shaped a new voice and an expanded approach for Malcolm. Jones asserts, "When Malcolm departed from the NOI amidst death threats and organizational hypocrisy, he illustrated once more that his search for religious understanding was still in process because he made the decision to embark on a spiritual journey, the Hajj."[4]

Regarding future reformed FLG members, the family legacy group established ideologies and practices that have influenced its members and affiliates who have joined the group. This impact extends to future generations of the family legacy group and members in the congregation associated with the members of the group. Black churches may not universally embrace the concept of trust and the acceptance of information based on association and influence, as observed in the congregation studied. Nevertheless, it is evident that individuals who hold significant positions of authority and wield power within the church, such as pillars of the congregation, play a crucial role in shaping the congregation's beliefs and attitudes. The significance of information in this context is not necessarily determined by its content alone but rather by the individuals who disseminate it and their degree of association with those who wield power and influence.

In this context, detaching is essential for those aiming for transformation, as it does not eliminate the chance to gather pertinent information. Rather, it offers a brief period of separation from individuals entrenched in a culture rooted in specific beliefs,

---

4. Jones, "Ideological and Spiritual Transformation," 427.

values, and norms, allowing for renewal, self-discovery, and the realization of one's potential. This detachment establishes the framework necessary to relearn how to build trust in God and others in a healthy manner.

One pushback to the initiation stage of detachment in the Black church context is the sense of belonging. The concept of belonging speaks to a feeling of being accepted and approved by a group or society.[5] Most individuals who associate themselves with members of the family legacy group benefit from their connection to the social power dynamic in the church. Connections to this medium foster social and congregational identity. It functions as an inclusionary all-access pass to rooms the unassociated member cannot access. Belonging to this group in most social and congregational contexts provides voice and consideration of thought and opinion on a given topic of discussion. Hence, detaching threatens social/congregational identity, status, access, voice, and opportunity.

Malcolm's and the members of the reformed family legacy group's experiences and encounters shed light on the consequences and effects of detachment as the initial step in the transformational process. The challenge that arises from detachment is social isolation and, in some cases, social or congregational ostracism. Detachment indicates that an issue exists within the social context of a specific environment. The only solution is to reframe how individuals still connected to the system perceive and frame those who attempt to challenge the status quo of a particular community. This underscores the power of social and cognitive frameworks in shaping beliefs and practices, mainly when influenced by charismatic leaders. This is crucial for a comprehensive understanding of transformative journeys.

Malcolm X and the select few from the family legacy group underwent the initial steps of the transformation process. Stepping outside their congregational/social space was risky. Now, in their individual spaces of encounter and experience, Malcolm and a select group of individuals once associated with the family legacy

---

5. *APA Dictionary of Psychology*, "Belonging."

group must exist on their own, detached and disconnected from what they once knew, from what once shaped who they were. Secondly, Malcolm's and the members of the reformed family legacy group's experiences and encounters shed light on the reality of physical detachment without initially separating from the organization's interpretational/hermeneutical philosophy. Thus, while physically separated from a specific community, the thought patterns and understandings of governance, polity, and biblical interpretation are still consistent with the teachings of the community once affiliated. For Malcolm, he is detached from the Nation yet connected to a working philosophy that does not fully speak to a transformed thought. The future reformed FLG members will be temporarily separated from the family legacy group. Still, their new experiences and encounters outside of the controlled congregational space are assessed in comparison to the embedded understandings that grounded their perceptions and interpretations for years.

Thus, physical separation without ideological detaching will not lay a needed foundation for authentic reshaping. Malcolm and future reformed FLG members show us that detaching, as a first stage, involves social distance and interpretational/psychological detoxification. This premise grounds Malcolm's social and religious positions and future reformed FLG members' pre-transformation. Hence, separation/detachment, physically and ideologically, is necessary as a starting point for transformation.

THE PROCESS—LIMINALITY

Undergoing the process of detaching from a system of thinking and behavior that was once trauma-based and oppositional can be challenging. While navigating this transformative process, these individuals moved beyond the spaces and mindsets where they first began to a sphere of what some would consider the unknown. This medium, understood as the unknown space, is interpreted as the liminal space. The notion of "liminality" is significantly associated with the work of anthropologist Victor Turner (d. 1983) and his numerous writings on ritual process and pilgrimage, such as "The Ritual Process: Structure and Anti-Structure" (1969) and "Process, Performance, and Pilgrimage: A Study in Comparative Symbology" (1979). For this book, I will reference Michelle Trebilcock's summation of liminality. According to Trebilcock,

> Liminality, or anti-structured sociality, is a unique phase that people move through in order to arrive at a new phase of structured sociality. It is a transitional middle, betwixt and between old and new structures of sociality. In its ritual context, liminality unfolds within itself, so that within this middle movement there are more dialectical unfoldings and complex social processes. As liminality is experienced outside of ritual, in de-ritualised societies, this dialectical process is an even more complex phenomenon, requiring careful attention to discern its dynamic movements.[6]

As evaluated by Trebilcock, liminality presents distinct points of intersection for Malcolm and future members of the reformed family legacy group. Although liminality serves as a conduit for identity transformation, Malcolm and future reformed legacy group members encountered a breach process, an interruption to what had previously been experienced as normative.[7] Although Malcolm had to reassess who he would be apart from the Nation, identity reshaping within a Black church context differed for future reformed legacy group members. Identity reshaping enables individuals to reshape their identities, beliefs, and behaviors to promote mutuality within the congregation and society. Still, it is crucial to consider identity radicalization's social and congregational implications.

While grappling with the unfamiliar poses a single obstacle in the congregational and social space, a more profound concern arises when personal identity modification becomes the result of detaching from one space to existing in this unknown space. Relating to the challenges for future reformed FLG members,

---

6. Trebilcock, "Towards a Theological Hermeneutic," 38.
7. Trebilcock, "Towards a Theological Hermeneutic," 39.

individuals who comprise the family legacy group associate themselves with the power dynamics within the church. Hence, an individual's identity marker is linked to the group they associate with within the church. When liminality is engaged, the process entails relinquishing a present identity marker to develop a new one. This implies surrendering one's identity and social connection.

When an individual enters a state of liminality, they temporarily set aside or abandon their existing identity, along with the social markers and relationships associated with it. This symbolic or actual shedding of status enables a transformation or renewal of the self. Liminality is frequently a collective and spiritual experience, facilitated through rituals, introspection, or significant life changes. This relinquishment of identity and social ties does not imply a permanent separation from the community but rather a temporary withdrawal or dislocation from previous roles and expectations. It is a transitional space that permits the reimagining and reconstruction of one's identity, often resulting in a new or altered self upon reintegration into society. This process is crucial to transformation in religious, cultural, or communal contexts, such as baptism, ordination, pilgrimage, or recovery from trauma, where identity undergoes profound reorientation.

This critical aspect of the transformation process may lead to hesitation in navigating the liminal space, as the reality of the process may revert to old thought patterns and social behaviors rooted in a need for acceptance. My assertion perceptively highlights a psychological and social issue within the process of transformation, specifically the conflict between progressing forward and regressing. This is especially pertinent in liminal spaces, which are naturally unstable, ambiguous, and anxiety-inducing. Scholarly literature strongly supports the notion that individuals may hesitate to fully enter or stay in the liminal space due to the discomfort it causes, opting instead to revert to familiar patterns. In their study, Taylor and Cranton delve into the theory of transformative learning from a constructivist approach, which is akin to the idea of liminality. They assert, "Transformative learning theory is based on the notion that we interpret our experiences in our own way, and that how we see the world is a result of our perceptions of our experiences."[8]

The desire for acceptance and belonging, linked to one's previous identity and social context, can create a strong pull backward. This resistance or fear of losing social connections can hinder transformation. This is particularly evident in collective settings like religious or communal environments, where identity is shaped by social validation. The psychological discomfort of being between identities or communities can lead to a retreat into the familiar, even when the familiar may be dysfunctional or limiting. To produce significant results, it is essential for the learning environment and facilitators to employ strategic and intentional methods to achieve the desired outcomes within the congregational or social setting.

Facilitators engaging with Black congregations and communities need to be aware of the profound historical, spiritual, and cultural influences that define the learning atmosphere. Brookfield contends that successful facilitation, especially in the context of adult and transformative learning, necessitates deliberate planning, cultural sensitivity, and reflective practice. He emphasizes that no method, regardless of its theoretical effectiveness, can be successful unless applied thoughtfully.[9] Learning methodologies such as Sankofa praxis, liberation-focused theological reflection, community learning circles, rituals, embodied practices, and asset-based empowerment models honor historical context, promote community empowerment, and foster environments that support healing and liberation.

A REFORMER'S TRANSFORMATION

Changes within the Black church, particularly those challenging power structures, often require a thorough reassessment of theology, leadership methods, and community involvement. This transformation can be achieved through prophetic defiance, theological

---

8. Taylor, *Handbook of Transformative Learning*, 5.
9. Brookfield, *Skillful Teacher*, 9.

shifts, and educational empowerment. Over time, members of reformed family legacy groups embraced a liberating theology that prioritized justice, fairness, and the empowerment of marginalized voices. Additionally, they were equipped and empowered through theological and biblical education, as well as social awareness, to enhance their capacity to resist oppressive systems within the church.

Rev. Dr. Cheryl Townsend Gilkes, sociologist and womanist theologian, examines the potential for transformation within Black churches. She asserts, "In the world of the sacred in any social context, one is able to find the widest variety of human constructions of meaning. The Black church is important because it has been the basis for ethnic identity and the context for mobilization for social change."[10] Similar to the transformative experiences of Malcolm X, a small group from the family legacy circle at Wayside Baptist Church began to evolve their perspectives through regular teaching, practice, and reflection. This transformation for the church group was sparked by the educational sessions. Although the majority attended Sunday services, only a few participated in the Bible study sessions. These weekly teachings were crucial for the family legacy members who joined the Bible study. During these sessions, participants posed questions, and the biblical teachings offered fresh insights and avenues for personal development.

Some of the younger members of the FLG began to discuss amongst themselves the frequent rotations of leaders, the inconsistencies within the congregation, and the need for growth among members and in spirituality. While they did not wish to challenge the existing power dynamics, they realized they desired more than they currently had. Consequently, attending these Bible study sessions and frequent learning summits created the desire for change and an opportunity for reformation. Interactions with those outside their congregation fostered a lens of what their overall congregational experiences could be.

Pastor White observed as members of the family legacy group began to rethink their perspectives on God, the Bible, the church,

---

10. Gilkes, "Sacred as the Basis," 35.

and its established governance. He saw several individuals from this group alter their attitudes and actions concerning the family legacy's role within the church. Gradually, these members started to move away from the ideology created by the family legacy group. They began to show respect, listen to, and work alongside the church's official leaders, rather than being influenced by the power dynamics of the family legacy group. Pastor White facilitated connections between those undergoing this transformation and external individuals and groups who supported their progressive journey. This transformation was nurtured through teaching and patience. Retreats and spiritual gatherings played a significant role in reshaping the mindset of several FLG members who were seeking to move beyond their survival mode.

Members of the reformed family legacy group concluded their journey of transformation by attending a weekend retreat. Although the distance of their trip was not as far as Malcolm's journey to Mecca, the experiences and encounters shared some similarities. For these individuals, the retreat served as a sacred environment for spiritual rejuvenation and enrichment for everyone present. Experiencing what they had learned in a setting outside their usual congregational environment was deeply impactful, allowing them to gain a refreshed understanding of God, themselves, fellowship, worship, praise, purpose, governance, and structure. People from various Christian denominations traveled from near and far to reconnect with God and each other, showcasing the power of this transformative experience. During this retreat, they also encountered a universal context, one that transcended denominational boundaries and was inclusive of gender, ethics, and social status classifications.

While relaxing at the retreat, members of the reformed family legacy group came together to discuss their reflections on their personal experiences. In this sacred environment, the day's social mantra was not rooted in perceptions, power struggles, past traumas, or survival strategies. They experienced a shift and started to envision what the church and community could become if everyone in the congregation embraced the transformation process together. For numerous reformed FLG members, tackling the external elements that contributed to issues within their congregations became a central concern. While these reformed members were cognizant of the ongoing tensions in their religious communities, they participated in activities that encouraged community engagement and outreach as a personal outlet.

Although their social activism was not as extreme as that of Black leaders and social groups in the 1960s, they did work alongside local government entities, such as the mayor's office and county freeholders, to aid marginalized individuals in their areas. However, their limited grasp of the social challenges impacting their communities made them reluctant to adopt a definitive stance without being thoroughly informed. Despite these obstacles, this group with a reformist mindset began to make a positive impact on their communities. As a result, they would eventually have to address the issues within their congregation directly. In his work, Anthony B. Pinn explores the concept of exodus language as a framework for transformation. In *Understanding and Transforming the Black Church*, he discusses how the themes of "exodus and exile" serve as influential tools in shaping the epistemological, cultural, and historical perspectives on the development of Black religious traditions.[11] He further notes that for some individuals, this notion of exodus was linked to a nationalistic call for emigration.[12]

I specifically mention Pinn because his interpretation of exodus language highlights the idea of movement or pilgrimage for members of the reformed family legacy group. This notion of departure signifies both leaving something behind and moving towards something new. Although their concept of "movement" does not imply a return to Africa, I can draw a similar interpretation of return.[13] However, it is more accurately understood not as a return, like Pinn's view, but as an introduction to the established concepts of governance, polity, and congregational practices. Like Malcolm, these reformed FLG members encounter the challenge

---

11. Pinn, *Understanding and Transforming*, 52.
12. Pinn, *Understanding and Transforming*, 53.
13. Pinn, *Understanding and Transforming*, 52.

of managing dualism within their congregational environment. They must reconcile their transformation with the necessity to present a viewpoint that aligns with their values while questioning the existing power dynamics. It is crucial to consider how these reformed members will function and engage with those they will reconnect with.

THE OUTCOME FOR MALCOLM

Malcolm underwent a profound transformation that allowed him to experience true Islam for the first time in his life. This internal transformation caused Malcolm to change significantly, leading him to adopt a new sense of purpose and to speak the words of Allah instead of Elijah Muhammad. For Malcolm, this experience altered the way he understood community. In America, a community for him was Black individuals and families, but here in Mecca, the community had a broader, more universal depiction. In this holy space, his blackness did not serve as an identifying marker comparable to his social experiences in America. In Mecca, Malcolm was another brother, gathered with other Muslims of like faith from varying ethnicities and social classes.

Malcolm underwent a transformation that was unique to him yet had a broader significance. Specifically, he was impacted personally by his newfound understanding of Islam. However, this understanding was not limited to his experience as a Black man; instead, it offered an interpretation that extended beyond race and was embraced by anyone who sought to connect with the oneness of God. In a way, Malcolm's experience paralleled that of the apostles at Pentecost, as both groups understood the importance of imagining community. For Malcolm, Mecca was a safe space for him to be and become. Although his fight against the ideology and practices of racism did not change, this new epistemology and transformation morphed his approach to assessing the American issue of racism as a global human rights issue.

With this premise in mind, Malcolm embarked on a mission to spread his message across neighboring nations. He emphasized the need to reevaluate the global perspective on the human rights crisis in America. As Les Payne notes,

> Malcolm argued that the fight for freedom and equality by Black Americans must become a global movement. By shining a light on racial oppression through a global lens, it would no longer be perceived as a domestic civil rights issue, but rather a violation of international human rights.[14]

Unlike other Black civil rights leaders of his time, Malcolm aimed to unite Black leaders worldwide to stand in solidarity for their community and hold America accountable for its mistreatment of its Black citizens. He urged leaders from the African diaspora to recognize that Black Americans were a part of their community and to work together to challenge American leaders and officials regarding the unjust treatment of their Black brothers and sisters in the United States.

Malcolm began to imagine. He pondered on how America could "radically alter itself. Malcolm believed that the whites from the younger generation, in colleges and universities, would see the handwriting on the wall and turn to a spiritual path of truth."[15] This thought process was Malcolm's hope to eradicate racism in America. Still, Malcolm knew that America, in her practice, would do whatever it took to maintain racism as a social status quo.

THE OUTCOME FOR REFORMED FLG MEMBERS

Before assessing the effects of transformation on the external world, it is essential to examine its influence on the reformed FLG members who have returned from their transformative experiences. This is where the premise diverges notably from Malcolm's situation. Unlike Malcolm, who came back to Harlem to create a new mosque and an interfaith group aimed at uniting against social and economic oppression faced by African Americans,

---

14. Payne, *Dead Are Arising*, loc. 437.
15. Payne, *Dead Are Arising*, loc. 348.

these reformed FLG members must now reenter their former environment. Although their separation from the past was only temporary, they now confront the challenge of reintegrating into their previous surroundings. While this issue is not frequently addressed in congregational discussions, it is vital to consider the psychological effects of this return. Specifically, how do members of reformed family legacy groups who have undergone transformation reconnect with a congregational setting still plagued by the same trauma they were freed from? Additionally, will their transformation endure, or is there a possibility of mental instability due to the ongoing trauma-based dynamics from non-reformed FLG members who continue to hold power in the church?

Reflecting about these reformed family legacy group members, I loosely compare it to the tale of Moses in the Old Testament. I particularly notice parallels in Moses' journey back to Egypt from Midian and the psychological challenges he encountered. Although Moses' story might not directly align with my themes of detachment, pilgrimage, or transformation, I perceive similar traits between Moses and the reformed family legacy group, especially in their psychological and social attitudes towards returning to a place where the same influential figures and social dynamics have remained constant since they left.

When examining the effects of transformation on reformed legacy group members, it is crucial to assess how their internal traits are altered after undergoing such changes. Does transformation encounter boundaries within specific settings, or does it operate as a force beyond temporal and spatial constraints? Reflecting on Moses' journey, these questions become pertinent. Although his divine encounter on the mountain is distinct from the transformation I am discussing, his reluctance to embrace the role of a liberator offers insights into self-evaluation. Similarly, members of the reformed family legacy group felt a slight unease when dealing with power structures within the church. Their retreat, which they viewed as transformative, left them hesitant to directly challenge the existing order, leaving congregants eager for change perplexed. Despite their personal transformation, their internal traits limited their capacity to engage with power dynamics and step beyond their own perspectives for the congregation's benefit.

When we think about transformation, we should consider whether we engage in it purely for our own benefit and satisfaction, or if we also aim to empower and free others through the experience. It is indeed a blend of both. This is why Malcolm is my ideal model. To me, Malcolm represents a courageous and independent thinker who is not influenced by propaganda. Such an individual might be perceived as a threat to the existing power structures because he cannot be swayed by lies and misinformation, which is why American society portrayed him as a revolutionary. Malcolm had a clear mission, which he pursued through various aspects of his life—to bring true Islam to America and to confront the oppressive systems of society. After spending several years under a misguided allegiance to the Honorable Elijah Muhammad, Malcolm was resolved to light the way for anyone willing to follow.

To those former family legacy group members who have undergone transformation, embrace the freedom you have attained. While not every reformed individual may choose confrontation as a method, it is essential to embrace the idea of freedom that the apostle Paul shared with the Galatian church when he wrote, "For freedom, Christ has set us free; stand firm therefore and do not submit again to a yoke of slavery."[16] Paul emphasizes to believers that the redemptive work of Christ frees them from both spiritual enslavement and oppressive systems. This liberation extends beyond the individual to encompass communal and ethical dimensions. It urges believers to live with integrity and bravery, resisting any return to conditions that undermine their inherent dignity bestowed by God.

To empower individuals who have experienced transformation within the Black church to persist despite fear, it is essential to provide both spiritual foundation and community support. Transformation, particularly when it involves questioning traditions, speaking truth to power, or embracing new leadership roles, can often lead to anxiety, opposition, and feelings of isolation. Here are

---

16. Gal 5:1.

two steps we need to take to maintain transformation. Firstly, we should strengthen theological foundations. When transformation is anchored in Scripture and faith traditions, it transcends personal change and becomes a divine mission. Secondly, we need to establish covenant communities of support. Without community, transformation can lead to exhaustion. People require safe and supportive environments to navigate fear, setbacks, and resistance.

For those who have undergone transformation to remain steadfast, the Black church must serve as both a refuge and a springboard, offering spiritual fortitude, community support, and practical guidance. The Black church's heritage is built on bravery in the face of adversity, from clandestine gatherings during slavery to the fight for freedom. This heritage should persist not only in theological teachings but also in the practice of lived discipleship. When this perspective is embraced by everyone who has transformed, we consciously create a pathway for anyone brave enough to embark on the journey toward transformation.

CHAPTER 7

Transformation's Impact on Congregational and Social Arenas

IN ASSESSING OUR GRASP of transformation, it becomes clear that the effects of transformation often impact those who have undergone the process differently than those who remain on its periphery. In numerous congregational and social contexts, individuals who experience transformation tend to distance themselves from their familiar surroundings to fully engage with the process. Onosu supports this notion, stating,

> Through the intentional process of cultural immersion and guided reflection, participants became aware of the need to reevaluate their perspectives, values, and beliefs. This often involved stepping away from familiar social and cultural environments, allowing them to engage deeply with new experiences that challenged their prior assumptions.[1]

Although detachment, pilgrimage, or retreat is temporary, those who participate in these activities must eventually return from their secluded experiences and rejoin the community or social settings of which they were once part. The difficulty in reintegrating lies in the change in an individual's role in an unchanged environment. When a person who has undergone transformation

---

1. Onosu, "Impact of Cultural Immersion," 7.

returns to an unchanged environment, such as a church, office, family, or community, they frequently face a mix of internal and external difficulties. What is the appearance of this, and is there the potential for change to affect those who are merely on the periphery? This chapter will explore the congregational and social challenges faced by Malcolm and the members of the reformed family legacy group as they reintegrate into these congregational and social environments.

WHAT HAPPENED WITH THOSE WHO TRANSFORMED IN THE CHURCH?

The teachings took hold effectively. The combination of new insights and spiritual retreats has brought a sense of renewal to several members of the family legacy group, who were previously entrenched in a rigid survival mindset. Although the pastor had to invest time and effort, change eventually took place. These individuals have descended from their metaphorical mountain and have rejoined the congregation. Returning to a social or congregational environment after undergoing personal change, particularly in spiritual, emotional, or ideological aspects, can be both freeing and difficult. This complexity is especially evident in congregational settings, where community identity, tradition, and shared beliefs are fundamental. Various elements are considered during this phase. Post-transformation, individuals might discover that their updated values or beliefs no longer completely match those of the community. This idea highlights the divergence of values and beliefs. There is often a tendency to reject hierarchical leadership in favor of more collective or shared leadership. Additionally, new theological or doctrinal views can disrupt the communal agreement.

After assessing the impact of certain members of the family legacy group who had transformed, it became evident that their attempts to operate within the church were met with resistance from those who adhered to their created survival system. Unfortunately, the positive changes resulting from the transformation were overlooked by those in the congregation, and those who embraced them viewed them as traitors by members of the family legacy group who sought to preserve their existing ways of survival. Although the reshaping process benefited some individuals, it served as a weakening agent to the power dynamics within the family legacy group.

Communities frequently perceive change as a threat, especially when it originates from within. Individuals who undergo transformation may experience feelings of alienation and marginalization within the broader community. Returning to a community often necessitates renegotiating one's role or identity. This process can be particularly challenging if the transformed individual previously held a leadership or respected position no longer wishes to engage in the same ministries or activities, or if their new outlook disrupts the established roles of others.

I remember a discussion I had with Pastor White. During a visit to the restroom, he overheard a conversation between two people. Although he could not catch every detail, Pastor White sensed tension between them. After leaving the restroom, he realized the two individuals were Sister Ruth, a member of the family legacy group, and Brother Charles, one of the members who had undergone transformation. Later that day, Pastor White received a call from Brother Charles. He provided a summary of his conversation with his aunt, explaining why he sought the information Pastor White had shared. Through this process, Charles discovered something new about both God and himself. He told his aunt that Pastor White's goal was not to gain power but to empower those he served to become better versions of themselves. While Sister Ruth was somewhat pleased with her nephew's newfound insight, she saw it as a loss for the group and a victory for the pastor.

With the introduction of new viewpoints, interpretations, and practical applications, members of the reformed family legacy group anticipated that their transformation would generate widespread excitement within the congregation. However, their conversations were confined to select groups both inside and outside the church, and they frequently faced ostracism, being labeled as supporters of the pastor. Rather than fostering unity, the transformation appeared to deepen divisions. The family legacy group demonstrated a skewed version of Paul Tillich's concept of ultimate concern. In chapter 1, part 3 titled "Our Search for Happiness and Self-Actualization," psychologist Tom G. Stevens, PhD, explores the philosophical perspective of Tillich in his book. Stevens highlights that Tillich's philosophy revolves around the concept that our ultimate concern is the most significant factor shaping our personality and life. He describes it as our personal "god" due to its tremendous influence. Tillich asserts that this ultimate concern dictates our values, beliefs, goals, emotions, and behaviors.[2]

When evaluating Tillich's stance on the actions of the family legacy group, the notions of power and control emerge as their central focus. Unlike the members of congregations, perception and trauma are not experienced in the same way. Trauma becomes evident in a church environment where they no longer have power and control. Because power and control are of utmost importance to them, they frequently overlook the negative impact of their actions. Lately, I remember having a conversation with a pastor who was dealing with challenges in the church where she works alongside members of the family legacy group. She expressed to me her disappointment and pain over a church that once flourished but is now facing a downturn. When she first joined the church, there were about seventy active members. After eight months, the number of attendees grew to two hundred and fifty. Everything seemed to be progressing well. However, confusion arose in the church when some FLG members noticed that congregants began approaching the pastor directly instead of going through them first.

Consequently, individuals who joined the church in search of love, growth, and acceptance became disheartened and eventually departed. While the reduction in membership and attendance affected the church both numerically and financially, the FLG members were solely concerned with maintaining power, influence, and control. Black churches have a rich history of family legacy groups focused on maintaining their governance and influence within the

---

2. Stevens, "Your Top Goal."

church. Nonetheless, there is a chance for both the church and the community to gain from a fresh perspective that emphasizes reciprocity and shared benefits. This change would necessitate a reassessment of power dynamics within the church, in line with the authorized offices and leadership structures specified in the official church polity. By doing so, it might be possible to break down factions within congregations linked to family legacy groups, such as the one that resulted in Pastor White's removal from Wayside Baptist Church.

Although Pastor White achieved significant successes during his three-year leadership, such as boosting membership, enhancing financial stability, and fostering a renewed community spirit, the family legacy group remained opposed to transformation. Consequently, crucial outreach programs focusing on trauma care, mental health, wellness, and nutrition were not prioritized at the church. After Pastor White's departure, the church unfortunately fell back into a state of congregational trauma. This situation underscores the necessity for change within the church to ensure comprehensive liberation for all its members. While the family legacy group at Wayside Baptist Church might think they triumphed in their disagreement with Pastor White, the situation is not as it seems. Even after his removal, Wayside spent almost three years without an elected leader, leading to the sale of property to keep financially afloat. This was a regrettable outcome of erratic leadership, ongoing disputes among church leadership groups, a drop in membership, and reduced income.

In numerous churches, the challenge of power and control emerges because some individuals do not have opportunities for authority in other areas of their lives. While the American social system has negatively impacted African Americans, my argument extends beyond them. It focuses on the social, economic, and educational barriers that hinder people from being considered for leadership positions outside the church. Often, a lack of recognition, esteem, and respect can influence a person's self-awareness and confidence. The church often provides leadership roles to those who have not had such opportunities in their social and professional settings. Any change within the church that modifies the power structure threatens a newly established identity that individuals are reluctant to relinquish. In these situations, actions are taken to remove the threat.

In comparing the story of Malcolm X to the church setting, it becomes clear that reaching a mutual understanding and acceptance of established traditions and practices is not a feasible solution. The Nation of Islam, the family legacy group, and the US government all aim to preserve the status quo and encourage adherence to their ideologies. Any attempt to challenge their authority is met with resistance, as they strive to eliminate any sources of empowerment that might lead to change. Consequently, Pastor White, who opposed their system within the church context, became a target.

As a result of this assessment, the internal conflicts among the unreformed members of the family legacy group led to actions that caused Pastor White's separation and the church's collapse. How does the desire to maintain power, even if it jeopardizes the sustainability of the congregation or society, influence social decision-making? Additionally, is there a link between African Americans, trauma, and authority? The relationship among these three elements is complex and varied. Historically, African Americans have faced systemic racism, discrimination, and oppression, leading to traumatic experiences within their communities. These traumas can stem from various interactions, including those with authority figures like law enforcement and government officials.

The African American community has endured a long history of mistreatment and ongoing discrimination from those in power. These experiences have led to feelings of distrust, fear, and injustice, which can have lasting effects on both individuals and the community. Recognizing and understanding these dynamics is crucial for promoting healing, addressing systemic issues, and fostering a sense of safety and well-being. Building trust, promoting equity, and tackling the root causes of trauma are essential steps toward creating a more just and inclusive society. As a result, an inclusive culture only seems advantageous when the social parameters of governance remain unchanged. While many community members may recognize the need for change, they often either leave in search of better opportunities or conform to the existing power structure through silence.

In the current environment, the church needs to operate in ways that extend beyond just the Sunday worship service. By acting as a resource center and establishing community development organizations, church members can receive the support they need to address their social shortcomings. Through these initiatives, church leaders can offer constructive alternatives that assist congregations in reorganizing themselves.

THE EFFECTS OF RESHAPING ON MALCOLM

In a similar vein, we can draw lessons from Malcolm X's experiences as he narrates his personal evolution in his autobiography. He considers how his encounters with white people in Mecca influenced him. At one stage, Malcolm articulated the view that "Islam is a Black man's religion"[3] and that white people did not visit Mecca. Nonetheless, he later expressed that his journey on the pilgrimage led him to reconsider his earlier views and let go of some of his previous assumptions. He even went as far as to state that "we were truly all the same (brothers)" because the shared belief in one God had removed any biases or prejudices from their minds, behaviors, and attitudes.[4]

Malcolm's experience on his pilgrimage altered his view of white Americans and instilled in him optimism for a more peaceful future. In his autobiography, he contemplates, "Each hour in the holy land grants me greater spiritual insight into the racial tension in America. It dawned on me that if white Americans embraced the Oneness of God, they could also accept the oneness of humanity, disregarding color."[5] Although the concept is com-

---

3. Payne, *Dead Are Arising*, loc. 440.
4. Malcolm X, *Autobiography*, 347.
5. Malcolm X, *Autobiography*, 347.

Transformation's Impact

mendable, the United States has a history deeply intertwined with racism. Eliminating colorism would necessitate the dismantling of the social construct of whiteness, a change that seems improbable.

Malcolm's change was undoubtedly beneficial. Like the reformed legacy group members, it primarily served Malcolm himself rather than America or the Nation of Islam. For some Muslims, Mecca was a place of immense importance, acting as a meeting point for those who wished to partake in this shared experience. I assess hajj similarly to a Christian retreat experience, where we return to our daily lives with fresh insights but still encounter the same challenges we left behind. In the same way, a changed Malcolm still had to deal with the reality of an unaltered white America. As a result, he persisted in his struggle against white supremacy.

Malcolm understood the significance of collaborating with Black leaders and organizations outside of Islam to pursue shared objectives of social, political, and economic advancement. His transformation led to the establishment of the Organization for Afro-American Unity, which served as a forum for Black individuals from diverse faiths and backgrounds to unite and strive for a brighter future. In his autobiography, Malcolm discusses the difficulties and intricacies of managing the dual challenge of being a Black Muslim in America. Malcolm states,

> It was a big order—the organization I was creating in my mind, one which would help to challenge the American Black man to gain his human rights and to cure his mental, spiritual, economic, and political sicknesses. Substantially, as I saw it, the organization I hoped to build would differ from the Nation of Islam in that it would embrace all faiths of Black men, and it would carry into practice what the Nation of Islam had only preached.[6]

Malcolm's evolution led to a new kind of tension with the Nation of Islam. The establishment of the OAAU (Organization for Afro-American Unity) served as his new base for combating white supremacy in America, while Muslim Mosque, Inc. (MMI)

---

6. Malcolm X, *Autobiography*, 322.

provided a place for Muslims to find spiritual freedom from Elijah Muhammad's teachings, which were seen as contrary to the Quran. The teachings of traditional Islam, which opposed the teachings of Elijah Muhammad, provoked members of the Nation. As DeCaro recounts, "'Let us fervently pray,' wrote one Algerian Muslim, 'that the readers of The Courier will not confuse the sect of Muhammad with that of true Islam. Islam does not preach hate; it does not preach racism; it only calls for love, peace, and understanding."[7] The reference to *The Courier* speaks to Elijah Muhammad's column in the *Pittsburg Courier*.

Malcolm X's conflicts with the Nation of Islam and the US government highlight the difficulties of confronting imperfect interpretations of Paul Tillich's ultimate concern. Throughout his life, Malcolm X challenged the core beliefs of both entities, both before and after his journey to Mecca. The Nation of Islam and the US government depend on structures that uphold their existing power, making them resistant to change. Malcolm's evolved viewpoint provides a means to maintain his identity while engaging with individuals and groups beyond his religious and ethnic affiliations, thereby challenging the systems of both the Nation of Islam and the US government.

WHICH SIDE ARE YOU ON?

The impacts of transformation on some levels are complex. In its simplest expression, I assert that transformation has varying effects. Transformation as a concept posits two opposing positions in congregational and social arenas: one exists as a protestor of transformation or a participator in transformation. As a protestor, one disagrees with the transformation process as a system and stands against what transformation has accomplished. Transformation to the protestor is not an act of progression but of congregational/social deconstruction. Transformation to the protestor dismantles the power dynamic. It destroys any hopes of sustaining

---

7. DeCaro, *On the Side*, loc. 146.

governances and practices supported by a singular group in the congregational/social space that does not support transformation.

In examining the Nation of Islam, non-reformed family legacy group members, and the US government, these entities exemplify protestors from my perspective regarding the two stances linked to transformation. From their viewpoint, transformation is not seen as progressive but rather as a step back from their objectives. The idea of negotiation contradicts their core values. I equate negotiation with mutuality, where both sides make concessions for the collective benefit. However, for these social and religious groups, any form of concession is a significant distortion of their goals. Mutuality does not align with their approach; instead, it serves as a metaphorical loophole that allows for further changes. From their perspective, transformation is not a viable alternative or an additional perspective but a direct assault on their established lifestyle and operations. Consequently, their approach was not to negotiate but to execute their plans.

We observed this concept in the dismissal of Rev. White and the murder of Malcolm X. Their deaths marked the end of their influence. In the case of Rev. White, any chance of rejuvenating both the congregation and the community vanished with his departure. Wayside was already known for being a contentious and dissatisfied congregation. The community had already lost its sense of hope. Rev. White's involvement might have changed the church's image and reputation if the family legacy group had sought to find a compromise. The issue with the family legacy group's stance and actions is that they failed to consider the negative impact their decisions would have on the church and the community. Churches consist of both salaried employees and volunteers who collaborate to enhance the congregation and the community they serve. Persistent conflicts and disputes within a congregation can deter involvement and backing. How can a church bring about positive change within its sacred spaces if transformation is never achieved?

For Malcolm, death was unavoidable. Attempts on his life had already occurred before his pilgrimage to Mecca. When Malcolm served as a national minister for the Nation of Islam, he posed a threat solely to the system. However, after severing ties with the Nation and undergoing a transformation, Malcolm became a danger to everyone! During his pilgrimage, Malcolm engaged with African countries to argue that America was guilty of human rights violations. Furthermore, upon his return to Harlem, he delivered a message of Islam that contradicted Elijah's teachings. This led to conflicts for Malcolm with both the Nation and the US government. Although there are theories suggesting the Nation was behind his assassination, what is certain is that Malcolm's position disrupted the status quo, and they could not permit him to live. Can you imagine how our world might have evolved if Malcolm were still alive? Can we picture the current state of the Black community if someone connected to Malcolm at that time had taken up his cause and continued his efforts? Regrettably, when Malcolm passed away, his work and mission perished with him.

As a participator in transformation, one engrosses oneself in the transformation process. Transformation is a conduit that links liberation to those who experience oppression and injustice. As a participator, transformation provides new ways to think, believe, and behave. As a participator, transformation reshapes and causes those who engage in its process an opportunity to experience a reality never thought possible. Malcolm X and the reformed FLG members represent this position about transformation.

Through their lens, transformation altered how they saw themselves and contributed positively to how others saw them. Referencing the reformed FLG members, a new interpretation of the church emerged through community outreach efforts. Before the transformation, most members limited community outreach through indoor flea market-styled events. Post-transformation, reformed members and Rev. White, prior to his dismissal, engaged in community-based initiatives that offered food vouchers, sanitary supplies for needy families, and options for one-on-one and group counseling sessions. Although non-reformists took issues with new ministry endeavors, those who made up the community, both Black and Hispanic, began to develop a newfound respect and appreciation for the church.

Transformation's Impact

Referencing Malcolm, his transformation reframed his religious and social agenda, which sparked a new secular activist group spearheaded by several young African Americans dedicated to his cause. Several progressive African American artists, playwrights, and writers welcomed Malcolm's departure from the Nation and anticipated his entry into civil rights causes.[8] One activist, Ossie Davis, believed Malcolm could serve as an ignitor for the civil rights movement. Davis thought Malcolm knew it would take more than civil rights legislation, jobs, and education to save the Black man. He knew that none of the traditional organizations that serviced Black folk, such as Black churches, colleges, sororities and fraternities, the NAACP, or the Urban League, were capable of doing what needed to be done.[9]

Ossie Davis offers a perspective that some Black churches seldom consider. Considering the issues plaguing our communities, e.g., social discrimination of Black and brown people, biased job opportunities, educational disparity, unjust policing, and a biased judicial system, to name a few, how do those outside our influence and purview assess our presence concerning the more significant issues impacting the community? Do our communities assess our presence as essential for the local Black church, or is the church seen as a proverbial placeholder? While congregations encounter internal issues, do Black churches ever move beyond tensions of power and control within the church and begin the more extensive work that negatively impacts the communities where they serve? Moreover, the bigger question is this: Do the interests of the community and the church align? And, if the church cannot resolve this internally, how can they unite for the greater good of the community beyond distributing food and clothing every other week?

---

8. Marable, *Malcolm X*, 239.
9. Marable, *Malcolm X*, 239.

When No One Leads the Church
Can Transformation Be Transformative?

Relating to the Black church, like any institution, it is not homogeneous, and reactions to transformation within it can vary widely. However, some common adverse reactions to transformation in the Black church might include resistance to change, fear of losing identity, division, conflict, loss of authority and power, generational differences, and external criticisms. Some church members resist transformation due to a deep attachment to power and control. Change can be unsettling and perceived as threatening to a particular group's identity and heritage. Transformation may be met with apprehension because it exposes deficiencies in an ideology intended to exist as a congregational status quo. Those who fear change from a survival modality to a transformative paradigm contribute to a church's inability to restructure a unique cultural and religious identity.

Transformation initiatives sometimes lead to division and conflict within the church community, as different members hold varying opinions about how the church should evolve. Disagreements over change can lead to internal strife and discord. Leaders and influential figures within the church may feel threatened by transformation, as it could challenge their established positions of authority and power within the community. Older congregation members may resist transformation, while younger members may be more open to change. This generational gap can lead to tension and conflict over the direction of the church. Transformation within the Black church may also face criticism from outside sources, including other religious institutions, community groups, and those who are merely resistant to change. External pressures can exacerbate internal resistance to transformation.

Although my evaluation is not universal, I frame my transformation assessment by considering my experiences as a congregational leader in conversations with other pastors, civic leaders, and occupational directors of varying ethnicities and spaces. While experiences suggest that transformation is unlikely in congregational spaces like Wayside Baptist Church, I am hopeful that transformation can be realized. While the family legacy group dynamic does not posit itself exclusively in the Black church context, its effects are crippling to churches, institutions, and organizational paradigms. I hope churches of all denominations, plagued with this congregational crisis, will embrace transformation, recognizing its mutual benefits to the church's overall mission. Transformation is interpreted as change and change in most spaces fosters a sense of discomfort. Still, family legacy group members can choose to face this challenge head-on and engage in an opportunity that can posit truth and positively reshape their beliefs and behaviors while remaining true to their values. Like Malcolm says,

> Despite my firm convictions, I have always been a man who tries to face facts and accept life's reality as new experiences and new knowledge unfold it. I have always kept an open mind, necessary for the flexibility that must go hand in hand with every form of intelligent search for truth.[10]

My main issue with using Malcolm as a comparable example in my earlier reference is that most members of family legacy groups are not truth-seekers. The assumption is that adaptability within the congregational setting depends on others conforming to the family's wishes, rather than the other way around. While I do not intend to criticize the Black church, truth-seekers generally adopt an open-minded approach, evaluating information before reaching a conclusion based on a single line of thought. I admire this perspective in relation to Malcolm. Even when he was committed to an incorrect ideology, he remained open and inquisitive about information. Malcolm simply wanted to discover the truth.

At the intersection of transformation and conflict lies our assessment of truth. In questioning transformation's ability to transform, what part, if any, does truth play in the equation? While knowing that truth for most is subjective, are there any objective forms of truth for the Black church that members of the family legacy group can consider when evaluating transformation as an

---

10. Payne, *Dead Are Arising*, loc. 441.

option in the congregation? Ronald Dworkin, in "Objectivity and Truth," asks,

> Is there an objective truth? Or must we finally accept that at the bottom, in the end, philosophically speaking, there is no "real" or "objective" or "absolute" or "foundational" or "fact of the matter" or "right answer" truth about anything, that even our most confident convictions about what happened in the past or what the universe is made of or who we are or what is beautiful or who is wicked are just our convictions, just conventions, just ideology, just badges of power, just the rules of the language games we choose to play, just the product of our irrepressible disposition to deceive ourselves that we have discovered out there in some external, objective, timeless, mind-independent world what we have actually invented ourselves, out of instinct, imagination and culture?[11]

I do not think objectivity is present in the Black Baptist church. Providing a vague explanation to address this question would suggest that objectivity is found in Black Baptist churches, which would not be accurate. Ideally, we assume that church members are focused on Christ, guided by the spirit, and unbiased in their decisions, fostering an environment where favoritism is not the norm. As a result, objectivity is lacking in the Black Baptist church, and most actions are influenced by subjectivity. We disguise our subjective motives with a facade of Christlikeness, but ultimately, our actions are driven by our emotions. Therefore, even what we perceive as transformation and its impact on change is subjective. I conclude that transformation is truly transformative only if a person actively participates in the process. The decision to engage in the transformation process is personal and, therefore, subjective.

My evaluation of transformation is somewhat distinct for Malcolm, akin to members of the family legacy group. For Malcolm, transformation sparked a worldwide surge. Malcolm X's promotion of human rights and equality for everyone, irrespective

---

11. Dworkin, "Objectivity and Truth," 87–139.

of race, initiated a change in his beliefs that expanded his perspective and message. By highlighting the shared humanity of all individuals and the necessity for unity among oppressed groups, he connected with many who were seeking a more inclusive approach to civil rights and social justice. By collaborating with other civil rights leaders and organizations, even those with differing ideological views, he contributed to forming a more cohesive effort in the fight for civil rights and racial equality. His legacy as a complex and influential figure remains a source of inspiration and debate.

Malcolm X and members of the reformed family legacy group experienced a profound transformation that deeply influenced their identities, even though it did not alter their social surroundings or some of the individuals they interacted with. Their journey illustrates that overcoming obstacles or reaching objectives can result in both personal and public development, a change in outlook, and adjustments in behavior. Not everyone connected to these congregational and social spaces undergoes transformation; it is reserved for those who actively seek it. This idea may challenge those who have transformed when they return to an environment that seems contrary to their life-altering experience.

Although Malcolm returned to America, he did not find himself in an environment unsupportive of his goals. For the reformed members of the family legacy group, the question arises: Can their transformation endure long enough for them to witness change in others? Can they thrive in a trauma-filled environment and serve as a lifeline for someone else? While I believe transformation is subjective, we all play a role as voices of reason and influence within our social circles. Those who have transformed must decide that those seeking change are worth the effort. When this mindset becomes firm, reformed members of the family legacy group can observe others undergoing the reshaping process. Although it may seem unlikely and impossible, I am confident that transformation is achievable and holds the potential to be a powerful catalyst for change and growth in both the church and the world.

Conclusion

FROM THE OUTSET OF this work, I have encouraged you to join me in a multifaceted dialogue, one that boldly juxtaposes the Nation of Islam during Malcolm X's years before his pilgrimage with the internal challenges faced by the Black Baptist church, particularly concerning the deep-rooted influence of family legacy groups. At first glance, these entities might seem entirely distinct. One represents an American Muslim movement forged in the fires of racial oppression and theological divergence from Sunni orthodoxy; the other is a Christian congregation with deep roots in African American religious tradition. However, upon closer examination, it becomes evident that beneath the surface, similar forces are at play: the drive to endure in adversarial environments, the inclination to build protective frameworks when trust in established systems wanes, and the challenge of letting go of these frameworks once they become integral to our identity.

For this reason, I have characterized survival modalities as "patterned clusters of normatively imbued ideas and concepts"[1] that not only direct actions but also shape the moral and political landscape in which individuals operate. The term "patterned clusters of normatively imbued ideas and concepts" is frequently associated with the definition of "ideology."[2] In this sense, ideologies are not merely random collections of beliefs; instead, they are structured systems of ideas and values infused with normative

---

1. Freeden, "Ideology."
2. Freeden, "Ideology."

content. These clusters encompass specific perspectives on power dynamics, social roles, and what is deemed normal or desirable within a society.

Essentially, these "clusters" create organized frameworks that assist individuals and groups in understanding their political and social environments and in justifying specific actions, policies, or institutions. These concepts are "normatively imbued" because they include judgments about what should be, rather than merely what exists. They influence attitudes, shape identities, and have the potential to either support or challenge current power structures.

Within both the Nation of Islam and the family legacy group, these modalities serve a practical purpose: they offer protection, foster unity, and provide a framework for interpreting the world. However, they also come with drawbacks. They can become rigid, solidifying into systems that resist mutual accountability, democratic engagement, and the collective governance that the broader community, whether it be the global ummah in Islam or the larger Baptist polity, has traditionally supported.

REVISITING THE JOURNEY THROUGH THE CHAPTERS

In chapter 1, we explored Malcolm X during the period before his pilgrimage to Mecca, a time when the Nation of Islam's exclusive beliefs and strict structures heavily influenced his thoughts and perceptions of power, authority, and identity. At this stage, the comparison to the family legacy group became evident: both entities function within a framework that opposes what they view as foreign or externally imposed systems of authority. For the Black Baptist church, this opposition is expressed through resistance to established governance—systems intended to support collective decision-making but instead seen as threats to their independence.

In chapter 2, our aim was to comprehend, rather than criticize, the social roots of family legacy groups. We explored the historical, relational, and congregational factors that initially drove these groups into a survival mindset. This endeavor was as much about

Conclusion

pastoral care as it was about analysis: to establish a secure environment where awareness could flourish, comfort could be nurtured, and social acceptance could be achieved. At this stage, education transcends the mere exchange of information; it involves fostering trust that encourages individuals to embrace vulnerability.

In chapter 3, attention turned to the transformative power of religious instruction, regular engagement, and the influence of external support networks. It was observed that transformation seldom happens in isolation. Malcolm's own transformation occurred when his theological perspective broadened, when he encountered a worldwide Muslim community that challenged the limited racial and doctrinal views he had previously held. For the family legacy group, a similar broadening is achievable when teaching is consistent, application is deliberate, and support reaches beyond the boundaries of the local congregation.

In chapter 4, we explored the concept of leadership, focusing on the importance of leaders embodying a behavioral ethic that aligns with the faith they profess. Leaders cannot anticipate change in others if their own actions contradict their message. We examined the interactions in Jeddah and Mecca, where the behavior of white and non-white Muslims illustrated how aligning actions with a shared faith can alter perceptions of authority and community. The lesson for the Black Baptist church is clear: leadership must be both doctrinally sound and relationally trustworthy to effectively guide family legacy groups beyond mere survival.

In chapter 5, the themes of Lent and pilgrimage were discussed, not simply as religious rituals but as deliberate acts of sacrifice, death, and renewal. Pilgrimage, in particular, served as a model for collective movement: a journey characterized by ritual, safe spaces, and community-building. These practices are not peripheral; they act as bridges that guide both individuals and congregations from old habits and ways of thinking to revitalized ways of living.

Chapter 6 explored the challenging phase following the journey: the return. Malcolm's experiences after his hajj demonstrated that undergoing a transformation does not shield one from the societal pressures of the environment to which they return. For members of reformed family legacy groups, reentry can activate old survival instincts. In this context, detachment becomes a practice, not a withdrawal from the community but a deliberate distance from the power dynamics that might draw one back into survival mode.

In chapter 7, we explored the social dynamics that arise when individuals who have undergone transformation return to a congregation still influenced by a survivalist mindset. We revisited the analogy with Malcolm, emphasizing that a personal transformation does not necessarily change the environment one returns to. The role of leadership is to nurture a congregational culture that perceives reformation not as opposition but as alignment with a collective ethic rooted in faith. We are left pondering this: What actions should we take, where can we find refuge, and is there any possibility for a fresh understanding of mutuality within the church and our social environments? Can all parties step away from their entrenched positions and come together on a shared platform?

THEOLOGICAL STAKES AND PASTORAL CHARGE

At the core of the issue lies the behavior of family legacy groups. My examination of the ideology held by members of the family legacy group, as initially outlined, serves as a crucial perspective for understanding their interactions. Although I am not implying that their attitudes and actions are beyond reconsideration, I interpret their behavior through the lens of their social upbringing. The way they continue to operate, which is comfortable for them, was in direct opposition to the methods and practices of the church after the local Black Baptist church appointed a permanent leader.

The problem isn't that their survival strategies lack logic or historical justification. Rather, the problem is that these strategies are based on emotional loyalty instead of theological truth; they are maintained not by the gospel's liberating message but by outdated patterns that have surpassed their initial protective role.

Conclusion

Just as the Nation of Islam's structure provided Malcolm X with a foundation but couldn't lead him to fully realize his calling, these survival strategies are insufficient to guide the Black Baptist church to fully realize its mission.

For those in leadership roles, the directive is unmistakable: transformation starts with us. Merely advocating for ethical behavior is insufficient; we must exemplify it in our actions. It's not enough to demand change from others; we must undergo personal transformation. While leadership that exemplifies humility, transparency, and responsibility won't instantly dissolve resistance, it has the possibility of gradually dismantling the barriers that have been constructed over generations in a survival mindset. We need to be open to acknowledging the pain that has led to a survival mindset while also ensuring that these past wounds do not dictate the congregation's future.

The Black Baptist church, its leadership, and its members must function in a manner that offers collaborative care and protection for each other. For this strategy to work, the church's ethos must be a sense of solidarity with a community of fellow pilgrims. Individuals in the church who represent the "Malcolms" of the congregation must witness pilgrim partners in the Black Baptist church who exhibit an ethic that aligns itself with a correct representation of what their faith context represents.

As a caring pastor, it is difficult to merely come to church, preach a sermon, collect a check, and repeat the process. The only way that real connection happens is through openness. When vulnerability is established, real connections are made, and feelings emerge. When a pastor begins to care about their congregants genuinely, it becomes difficult to see their potential yet remain subject to a governing power dynamic. When a congregational leader encourages members to consider a reshaping process, the intention exists to move the congregational leader to help that member become the best version of themselves. Those who wield power often interpret a congregational leader's intention as self-seeking. To a degree, it is, but what some may consider as self-seeking is a desire to help. Again, real association exists as the byproduct of closeness, and closeness does not materialize in any relationship without mutual openness.

THE BLACK BAPTIST CHURCH AND BEYOND

While this book is rooted in the context of a particular urban-based Black Baptist church, the patterns we have explored are not exclusive to it. Any religious/social community that has experienced historical trauma, extended marginalization, or deeply-rooted power structures can adopt survival strategies. The insights shared here regarding awareness, education, leadership, rituals, journeys, reintegration, and reconciliation are relevant wherever the desire for transformation encounters the resistance of established systems. While my premise aims to inspire hope, it is crucial to recognize the role of influential voices within our congregational/social environments and how they shape our perceptions and practices in social and congregational settings. This influences our engagement with congregational and social life, potentially confining us to misguided or oppositional conditions influenced by sociocultural factors, or alternatively, allowing us to redefine our ideals for effective functioning and governance within society and the local Black Baptist church. By embodying these ideals with a sense of mutuality, we can create an environment that promotes inclusivity and fairness for everyone.

Open dialogue within congregational/social spaces is not just needed; it is necessary. Dr. Traci C. West, in *Disrupting Christian Ethics: When Racism and Women's Lives Matter*, speaks to the importance of dialogue. She writes, "Community cooperation across cultural and religious boundaries depends upon our ability to dialogue with one another."[3] In some cases, when groups are open, establishing a resolution and entering a conversational space can be a practical starting point for collective community building.

While no religious tradition has all the answers, many within the church and the public square struggle with the lack of emphasis and practices of ethics as a foundational extension of our faith

---

3. West, *Disruptive Christian Ethics*, loc. 126.

Conclusion

in the Black Baptist church. Nullifying the "doing" component of the christological message and mission translates to a partial faith understanding of its hermeneutic and practice. The historical Jesus presented to us in the biblical canon was effective because of what he said and did. Thus, what he said aligned with what he did. This medium implies that our faith practice must align with our faith understanding, moving us to make some spiritual and behavioral modifications. James Baldwin echoes this sentiment in his book entitled *Nobody Knows My Name*. Baldwin writes,

> Any real change implies the breakup of the world as one has always known it, the loss of all that gave one an identity, the end of safety. And at such moment, unable to see and not daring to imagine what the future will now bring forth, one clings to what one knew, or thought one knew; to what one possessed or dreamed that one possessed. Yet, it is only when a man is able, without bitterness or self-pity, to surrender a dream he has long cherished or a privilege he has long possessed that he is set free—he has set himself free—for higher dreams, for greater privileges.[4]

Baldwin reminds us that genuine change is not merely an outward alteration; it involves unraveling the core of our self-perception. His words challenge us with the reality that transformation requires letting go, and this act of surrender can feel like a loss, or even akin to death. However, within this process of breaking open lies potential. By releasing what we hold onto, be it the illusion of security, the comfort of identity, or the hold of privilege, we create room for something greater to arise.

Embracing change wholeheartedly demands bravery to remain in the unknown without retreating to what is familiar. However, the freedom Baldwin speaks of is not granted by the world; it is a liberation one attains by letting go of the urge to hold on. Thus, change is not about forsaking our true selves but about broadening our horizons, envisioning new identities, greater security, and elevated aspirations for human potential.

4. Baldwin, *Nobody Knows My Name*, 117.

SCRIPTURAL ANCHOR

At this point, I revisit the verse that has shaped my outlook: "All Scripture is inspired by God and is beneficial for teaching, reproof, correction, and training in righteousness."[5] The term "all" in this context is broad. It encourages us to acknowledge God's truth wherever it appears, within the Christian Scriptures, in the prophetic voices of other religious traditions, and in the transformative experiences of individuals. The aim is not to blend theological systems but to allow God's truth, in whatever form it manifests, whether in the narratives of prophets and apostles, the hard-won wisdom of our elders, or the journey of someone like Malcolm X, whose path reminds us that no belief system, no matter how flawed, is beyond the possibility of transformation.

As both a Christian and a researcher, I uphold this assertion, though I recognize there might be resistance to accepting any interpretation of divine truth that is presented outside the biblical canon linked to the Christian church. My chosen verse explicitly mentions that Scripture is "God-inspired," a concept traditionally aligned with what we consider our Holy Bible. Despite the advancements in technology and artificial intelligence as educational tools, I remain unconvinced that some urban-based Black Baptist churches specifically, or the Christian church in general, is prepared to embrace an interpretation of sacred Scripture in any format other than the one they have long been familiar with.

Restricting our view of what constitutes inspirational or sacred literature solely to the Christian canon limits our understanding of how human societies find meaning, experience transcendence, and derive ethical guidance. Texts from outside the Christian canon, whether they originate from other religions, philosophical traditions, or even secular sources, offer profound insights into the human experience, including themes of suffering, justice, community, and hope. By confining inspiration to the Bible alone, we overlook this rich reservoir of wisdom.

---

5. 2 Tim 3:16, NIV.

Conclusion

"Sacred" doesn't have to be limited to religious contexts; it can also encompass social, cultural, or existential dimensions. For instance, African American spirituals, indigenous oral traditions, or influential speeches like Martin Luther King Jr.'s "Letter from a Birmingham Jail" serve as sacred by offering guidance, healing, and inspiration to communities. Broadening the concept of sacred texts beyond the Christian canon encourages empathy and dialogue among different cultures and religions, which is essential in a diverse society. This approach helps prevent exclusivity and allows for the possibility of shared values across various traditions.

In liberationist and contextual theologies, the concept of "text" is broadened to encompass lived experiences, historical events, and community stories. For instance, Black, feminist, and postcolonial theologians highlight that sacred knowledge is derived from the experiences of struggle, survival, and storytelling, just as it is from traditional Scripture.

If this is our universal perspective, then as a person of color whose heritage and ancestry extend back before the advent of Americanized/Western Christianity, the transatlantic slave trade, and in some respects, the development and dissemination of our scriptural canon, I claim that our perception of God is entirely connected with African religious and ritual traditions that existed before Islam, Christianity, and even Judaism. Does our religious connection to what we define as God originate with the empire, or can we affirm that the God of the universe has always transcended our religious and denominational ties from the outset? If this is our assertion, then we must expand our comprehension of sacred texts and the various ways in which the God of the universe seeks to reveal Godself and interact with those who choose to connect with God.

A Final Vision

Given that objectivity is absent in the Black Baptist church, how can leaders work together to build connections that guide congregations through a transformative journey? More importantly, how do leaders operate in congregational settings that resist change? Is there even a solution? As mentioned earlier, change is subjective, meaning that transformation is a personal decision. What steps can we take when we wish for something for others that they do not want for themselves?

Although I earnestly wish to devise a strategy to address this congregational issue, which is commendable, I have come to terms with the possibility that a solution might not be attainable in all congregational spaces. While I can theorize endlessly, as a practitioner, I must eventually descend from the mountain and continue my work in the valley. With this perspective, perhaps presenting this work will initiate the dialogue. Once the conversation begins and feasible options are considered, both congregants and leaders can uncover practical theories and practices, engaging the church in the transformation process.

If I could leave you with a single image, it would be this: a group of people traversing a bridge. On one side is a state of mere survival, characterized by familiar barriers, internal allegiances, and a wary attitude toward outsiders. On the opposite side is a state of renewal, marked by open spaces of mutual trust, collaborative leadership, and actions that align with the spirit of Christ. Crossing this bridge is challenging. It demands sacrifice, the willingness to let go, and leaders who are willing to take the first step and continue moving forward, even when the journey is lengthy. Yet, on the other side, there is liberation.

Let us find the bravery to embark on that journey. May we possess the humility to gain wisdom from any life, tradition, or testimony that reflects genuine transformation, and may our communities, once they have made the crossing, never again settle for mere survival when God's promise is resurrection.

Bibliography

APA Dictionary of Psychology. "Belonging." Updated April 19, 2018. https://dictionary.apa.org/belonging.
———. "Dissonance Reduction." Updated April 19, 2018. https://dictionary.apa.org/dissonance-reduction.
———. "Interdependence Theory." Updated April 19, 2018. https://dictionary.apa.org/interdependence-theory.
———. "Mutuality." Updated April 19, 2018. https://dictionary.apa.org/mutuality.
Baldwin, James. "Faulkner and Desegregation." Ch. 7 in *Nobody Knows My Name: More Notes of a Native Son*. New York: Dial, 1961.
Banks, Robert, and Bernice M. Ledbetter. *Reviewing Leadership: A Christian Evaluation of Current Approaches*. 2nd ed. Grand Rapids: Baker Academic, 2016.
Barnes, Sandra L. "Black Church Culture and Community Action." *Social Forces* 84.2 (2005) 967–94. academic.oup.com/sf/article-abstract/84/2/967/2235468.
Brookfield, S. D. *The Skillful Teacher: On Technique, Trust, and Responsiveness in the Classroom*. 2nd ed. Hoboken, NJ: Jossey-Bass, 2006.
Cleveland Clinic. "What Is the Fight, Flight, Freeze or Fawn Response?" July 22, 2024. https://health.clevelandclinic.org/what-happens-to-your-body-during-the-fight-or-flight-response.
Collins-Kreiner, Noga. "Researching Pilgrimage: Continuity and Transformations." *Annals of Tourism Research* 37.2 (2010) 440–56.
Créton, Hans, et al. "A Systems Perspective on Classroom Communication." In *Do You Know What You Look Like? Interpersonal Relationships in Education,* edited by Theo Wubbels and Jack Levy, 1–12. London: RoutledgeFalmer, 1993.
Curtis, Edward E., IV. *Islam in Black America: Identity, Liberation, and Difference in African-American Islamic Thought*. Albany: State University of New York Press, 2002.
Dagnini, J. K. "Marcus Garvey: A Controversial Figure in the History of Pan-Africanism." *Journal of Pan-African Studies* 2.3 (2008) 198–208. http://www.

jpanafrican.org/docs/vol2no3/MarcusGarveyAControversialFigureIn TheHistoryOfPanAfricanism.pdf.

DeCaro, Louis A., Jr. *On the Side of My People: The Religious Life of Malcolm X*. New York: NYU Press, 1997. Kindle ed.

Dickerson, Dennis C. "Our History." AME Church. https://www.ame-church.com/our-church/our-history/.

Dixie, Quinton Hosford. "Black Baptists." Oxford Bibliographies, July 25, 2023. doi.10.1093/obo/9780190280024-0121.

Dworkin, Ronald. "Objectivity and Truth: You'd Better Believe It." *Philosophy & Public Affairs* 25.2 (1996) 87–139.

Eade, John, and Michael J. Sallnow, eds. *Contesting the Sacred: The Anthropology of Christian Pilgrimage*. Eugene, OR: Wipf & Stock, 2013.

Encyclopedia Britannica. "Systems Theory." Last updated Sept. 26, 2025. https://www.britannica.com/topic/systems-theory.

Fairholm, Matthew R. "Leadership and Organizational Strategy." *The Innovation Journal: The Public Sector Innovation Journal* 14.1 (2009) 1–16.

Farley, Margaret A. *Just Love: A Framework for Christian Sexual Ethics*. New York: Bloomsbury Academic, 2008.

Flynt, Sean. "Theology of Mutuality Can Rebuild a Declining Church, Ketcham Says." Samford University, Dec. 10, 2019. https://www.samford.edu/arts-and-sciences/news/2019/Theology-ofMutuality-Can-Rebuild-Declining-Church-Ketcham-Says.

Freeden, Michael. "Ideology." Routledge Encyclopedia of Philosophy, Taylor and Francis, 1998. https://www.rep.routledge.com/articles/thematic/ideology/v-1.

Freire, Paulo. *Pedagogy of the Oppressed*. Translated by Myra Bergman Ramos. New York: Bloomsbury, 2014. Kindle ed.

Gilkes, Cheryl. *If It Wasn't for the Women: Black Women's Experience and Womanist Culture in Church and Community*. New York: Orbis, 2000.

———. "The Sacred as the Basis for Human Creativity and Agency in the Black Church." *Trotter Review* 10.2 (1997) 12.

Green, Ronald, M. *Religion and Moral Reason: A New Method for Comparative Study*. Oxford: Oxford University Press, 1988.

Greenia, George D. "What Is Pilgrimage?" *International Journal of Religious Tourism and Pilgrimage* 6.2 (2018) 3. https://arrow.tudublin.ie/ijrtp/vol6/iss2/3/.

Gutiérrez, Gustavo. *A Theology of Liberation: History, Politics, and Salvation*. New York: Orbis, 1973.

Hill-Smith, Connie. "Cyberpilgrimage: The (Virtual) Reality of Online Pilgrimage Experience." *Religion Compass* 5.6 (2011) 236–46.

Hollenbach, David. *The Common Good and Christian Ethics*. Cambridge: Cambridge University Press, 2002.

hooks, bell. "Engaged Pedagogy." In *Teaching to Transgress: Education as the Practice of Freedom*. New York: Routledge, 1994.

Bibliography

Horowitz, Juliana, et al. "Views of Racial Inequality in America." Pew Research Center's Social & Demographic Trends Project, Apr. 9, 2019. https://www.pewresearch.org/social-trends/2019/04/09/views-of-racial-inequality/.

Hunter, Rodney J., "Preaching Lent: Challenges and Opportunities." *Journal for Preachers* 43.2 (2020) 10.

James, Paul, and Manfred Steger, eds. *Ideologies of Globalism*. Globalization and Culture 4. Thousand Oaks, CA: Sage, 2010.

Jones, Trevin. "The Ideological and Spiritual Transformation of Malcolm X." *Journal of African American Studies* 24.3 (2020) 417–33. https://www.jstor.org/stable/48737244.

Kearney, Susan. "What Are the 4 Themes of Lent?" Christian.net, Feb. 29, 2024. https://christian.net/spiritual-growth/what-are-the-4-themes-of-lent/.

Leary, Joy DeGruy, and Randall Robinson. *Post Traumatic Slave Syndrome: America's Legacy of Enduring Injury and Healing*. Stone Mountain, GA: Joy DeGruy, 2018.

Lincoln, C. Eric. "The Power in the Black Church." *Cross Currents* 24.1 (1974) 3–21. http://www.jstor.org/stable/24457876.

Lincoln, C. Eric, and Lawrence H. Mamiya. *The Black Church in the African American Experience*. Durham, NC: Duke University Press, 1990.

———. "The Dialectical Model of the Black Church." In *Down By the Riverside: Readings in African American Religion (Religion, Race, and Ethnicity)*, edited by Larry Murphy, 329–38. New York: NYU Press, 2000.

Marable, Manning. *Malcolm X: A Life of Reinvention*. New York: Penguin, 2011. Kindle ed.

Martin, Richard C. "Pilgrimage: Muslim Pilgrimage." Encyclopedia of Religion, 1987. https://www.encyclopedia.com/environment/encyclopedias-almanacs-transcripts-and-maps/pilgrimage-muslim-pilgrimage.

Maxwell, John C. "The 25–50–25 Principle of Change." Maxwell Leadership, Feb. 26, 2019. www.johnmaxwell.com/blog/the-25-50-25-principle-of-change/.

Merton, Thomas. *New Seeds of Contemplation*. New York: New Directions, 2007.

Mezirow, Jack. *Learning as Transformation: Critical Perspectives on a Theory in Progress*. Hoboken, NJ: Jossey-Bass, 2000.

———. "Transformative Learning Theory." Ch. 8 in *Contemporary Theories of Learning: Learning Theorists . . . In Their Own Words*, edited by Knud Illeris. New York: Routledge, 2018.

Mohamed, Besheer, et al. "Religious Practices." Faith Among Black Americans 4. Pew Research Center, Feb. 16, 2021. https://pewrsr.ch/2ZooxDW.

Onosu, Gloria. "The Impact of Cultural Immersion Experience on Identity Transformation Process." *International Journal of Environmental Research and Public Health* 18.5 (2021) 2680. https://doi.org/10.3390/ijerph18052680.

Paul, Laurie Ann. *Transformative Experience*. Oxford: Oxford University Press, 2014.

Payne, Les, and Tamara Payne. *The Dead Are Arising: The Life of Malcolm X*. New York: Liveright, 2020. Kindle ed.
PBS. "Timeline of Malcolm X's Life." https://www.pbs.org/wgbh/americanexperience/features/malcolmx-timeline-malcolm-xs-life/.
Pinn, Anthony B. *Understanding and Transforming the Black Church*. Eugene, OR: Cascade, 2010.
Ransford, Elizabeth Hoffman. "Sacred Spaces, Public Places: The Intersection of Religion and Space in Three Chicago Communities, 1869–1932." PhD diss., Loyola University Chicago, 2010.
Richardson, Ronald W. *Creating a Healthier Church: Family Systems Theory, Leadership, and Congregational Life*. Minneapolis: Fortress, 1996.
Rudy, Kathryn M. "A Guide to Mental Pilgrimage: Paris, Bibliothèque de L'Arsenal Ms. 212." *Zeitschrift für Kunstgeschichte* 63.4 (2000) 494–515.
Russo, Nicholas V. "The Early History of Lent." The Center for Christian Ethics at Baylor University. *Lent* (2013) 18–26. https://ifl.web.baylor.edu/sites/g/files/ecbvkj771/files/2022-12/LentArticleRusso.pdf.
Schellenberg, Susanna. "Perceptual Particularity." *Philosophy and Phenomenological Research* 93.1 (2016) 25–54. https://doi.org/10.1111/phpr.12278.
Schwarz, Norbert, and Herbert Bless. "Constructing Reality and Its Alternatives: An Inclusion/Exclusion Model of Assimilation and Contrast Effects in Social Judgment." In *The Construction of Social Judgment*, edited by Leonard L. Martin and Abraham Tesser, 217–45. Hillsdale, NJ: Lawrence Erlbaum Associates, 1992.
Smith, Archie. "The Relational Self and Social Transformation." Ch. 3 in *The Relational Self: Ethics and Therapy from a Black Church Perspective*. Nashville: Abingdon, 1982.
Steinke, Peter L. *How Your Church Family Works: Understanding Congregations as Emotional Systems*. Lanham, MD: Rowman & Littlefield, 2006. Kindle ed.
Stevens, Tom G. "Your Top Goal in Life as a Major Cause of Happiness or Unhappiness." In *You Can Choose to Be Happy: Rise Above Anxiety, Anger, and Depression with Research Results*. Reading, UK: Wheeler-Sutton, 2010. https://home.csulb.edu/~tstevens/h13topgo.htm.
Taylor, Edward W., and Patricia Cranton. *The Handbook of Transformative Learning: Theory, Research, and Practice*. Hoboken, NJ: Jossey-Bass, 2012.
Thurman, Howard. "Every Man Must Decide." Pt. 2, ch. 13 in *Meditations of the Heart*. Boston: Beacon, 1999. Kindle ed.
Tillman, J. Jeffrey. *An Integrative Model of Moral Deliberation*. London: Palgrave Macmillan, 2016.
Tollifson, Joan. *Nothing to Grasp*. Oakland, CA: Non-Duality, 2012.
Townes, Emilie M. *Womanist Ethics and the Cultural Production of Evil*. New York: Palgrave Macmillan, 2007.
Tractenberg, Paul L. "A Tale of Two Deeply Divided NJ Public School Systems." NJ Spotlight News, Dec. 13, 2013. https://www.njspotlightnews.

Bibliography

org/2013/12/13-12-30-a-tale-of-two-deeply-divided-new-jersey-public-school-systems/.

Trebilcock, Michelle. "Towards a Theological Hermeneutic for Contexts of Change: Love in Liminality." PhD diss., Charles Sturt University, 2015.

Trull, Joe E., and James E. Carter. *Ministerial Ethics: Moral Formation for Church Leaders*. 3rd ed. Ada, MI: Baker Academic, 2011.

Wang, Wendy. "The Decline in Church Attendance in COVID America." Institute for Family Studies, Jan. 20, 2022. https://ifstudies.org/blog/the-decline-in-church-attendance-in-covid-america.

Warfield, Heather A. "Quest for Transformation: An Exploration of Pilgrimage in the Counseling Process." *VISTAS* 1 (2012) 35.

Warfield, Heather A., et al. "The Therapeutic Value of Pilgrimage: A Grounded Theory Study." *Mental Health, Religion & Culture* 17.8 (2014) 860–75. doi.org/10.1080/13674676.2014.936845.

West, Traci C. *Disruptive Christian Ethics: When Racism and Women's Lives Matter*. Louisville, KY: Westminster John Knox, 2006. Kindle ed.

Wijeyesinghe, Charmaine L., and Bailey W. Jackson, eds. *New Perspectives on Racial Identity Development: Integrating Emerging Frameworks*. 2nd ed. New York: New York University Press, 2012.

X, Malcolm, et al. *The Autobiography of Malcolm X: As Told to Alex Haley*. New York: Ballantine, 1964.

www.ingramcontent.com/pod-product-compliance
Lightning Source LLC
Chambersburg PA
CBHW072145160426
43197CB00012B/2253